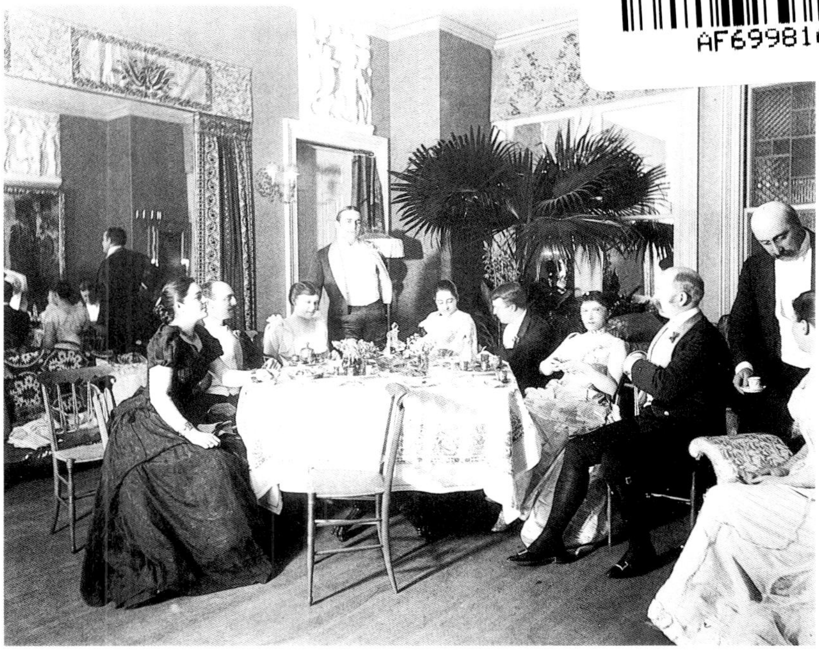

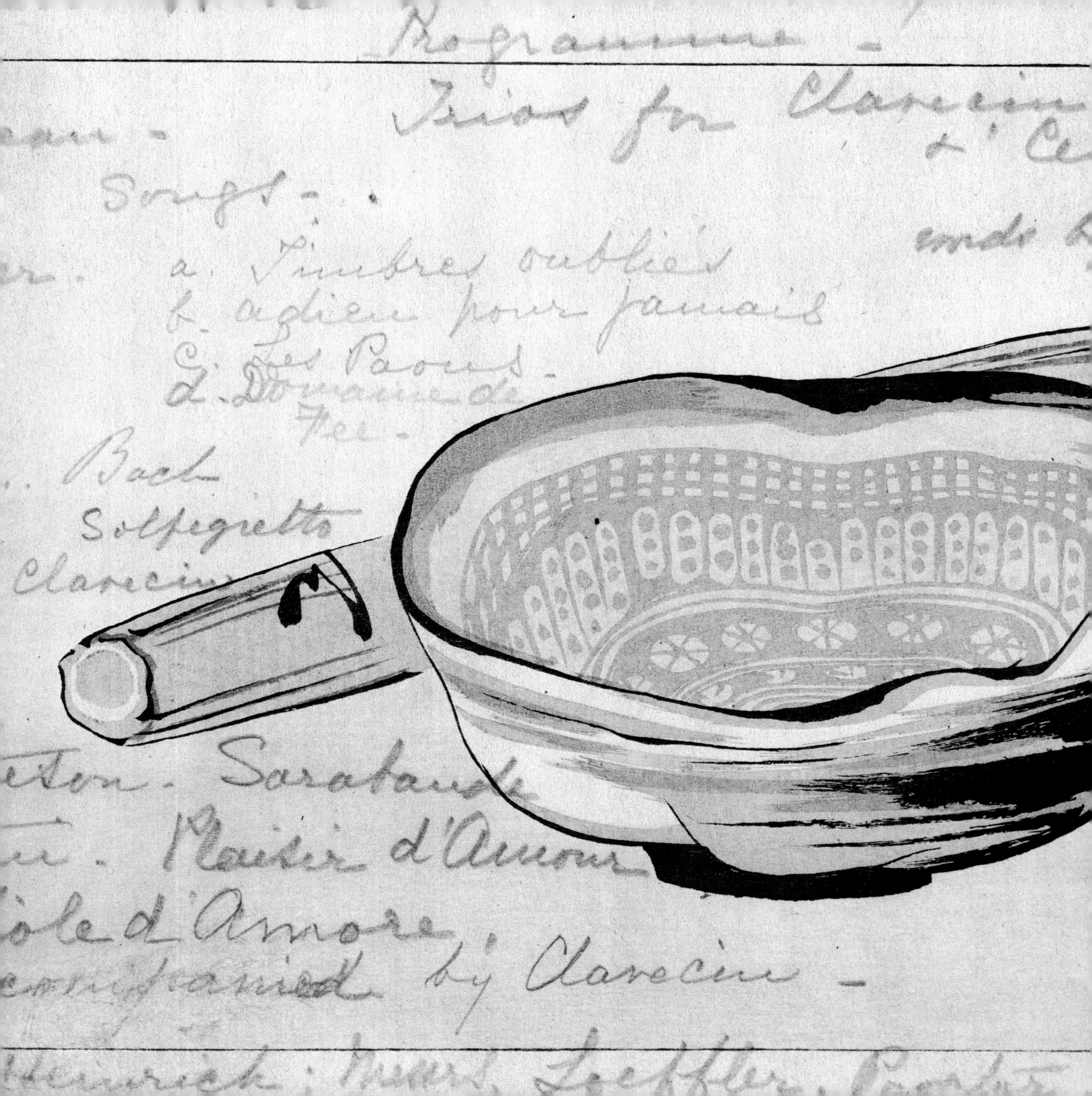

Programme
Trios for Clavecin
Songs
a Timbres oubliés
b adieu pour jamais
c Les Paons
d Domaine de Fée
Bach
Solfegietto
Clavecin
Sarabande
Plaisir d'Amour
Viole d'Amore
accompanied by Clavecin

LEE MINGWEI

THE LIVING ROOM

Jennifer R. Gross   Lewis Hyde

Isabella Stewart Gardner Museum   Boston   Massachusetts

This book is published in conjunction with the exhibition:
Lee Mingwei
The Living Room

February 18–April 30, 2000, at the Isabella Stewart Gardner Museum, Boston

Published by the Trustees of the Isabella Stewart Gardner Museum
Two Palace Road, Boston, Massachusetts 02115

Cover: Installation view, *Christ Bearing the Cross* (after Giovanni Bellini, died 1516).
Photograph by David Bohl, 1993.
Inside front cover: The Gardners entertaining guests in the music room of their home at 152 Beacon Street before the Myopia Hunt Club Ball, 1891.
Inside Back cover: Isabella Stewart Gardner on lawn at Green Hill, 1902.
Endpapers: Green Hill Concert Programs, May 10, 1900.

Photographs are courtesy of Lombard/Freid Fine Art, New York, New York; Mr. Glory Yeh; Cleveland Center for the Arts, Cleveland, Ohio; The Whitney Museum of American Art, New York, New York.

Photographers: Cristian Alexa, David Bohl, G. Hirose, Anita Kan, Joseph Pratt.

Designer: Ruth Abrahams
Typefaces: Frutiger and Scala
Printer: Meridian Printing, East Greenwich, Rhode Island

Distributed by University Press of New England, Hanover and London

ISBN 0-914660-13-6
Library of Congress Cataloging-in-Publication Data
Gross, Jennifer R.
Lee Mingwei: The living room / Jennifer R. Gross, Lewis Hyde.
p. cm.
Catalog of an exhibition held at the Isabella Stewart Gardner Museum, Boston, February 18–April 30, 2000.
ISBN 0-914660-13-6
1. Lee, Mingwei, 1964-Living room--Exhibitions. 2. Installations (Art)--Taiwan--Exhibitions. I. Lee Mingwei, 1964- II. Hyde, Lewis, 1945- III. Isabella Stewart Gardner Museum. IV. Title.
N7349.83.L43 A7 2000
709' 04'07--dc21 99-089887

Public and artist programming is made possible by the Barbara Lee Program Fund, the Lila Wallace–Reader's Digest Fund, and the National Endowment for the Arts. Major support for *Eye of the Beholder* programs has been provided by The Pew Charitable Trusts, the Stratford Foundation, The Boston Foundation, GTE, and the Clipper Ship Foundation.

A portion of the Museum's general operating funds for this fiscal year has been provided through grants from the Institute of Museum and Library Services, a Federal agency; and the Massachusetts Cultural Council, a state agency that receives support from the National Endowment for the Arts.

CONTENTS

PREFACE

The artist-in-residence program at the Gardner Museum continues the tradition of supporting living artists established by Isabella Stewart Gardner. During her lifetime she patronized artists as varied as John Singer Sargent, Henry James, and Ruth St. Denis, supporting their creative work.

Lee Mingwei, during his residency at the Gardner in the summer of l999, absorbed the Museum's intimate nature and perceived it as a lively, animated, organic whole. Thus he conceived his exhibition. By involving members of the Museum family, Lee creates a living extension of Isabella's tradition of hospitality. Visitors to the exhibition experience the intimate process of sharing and entertaining that was such a vital part of Isabella Gardner's Fenway Court. As a visitor to *The Living Room*, you are invited to engage in an exchange of ideas and reflections with members of the Museum governance and staff. It is the artist's hope, and the Museum's also, that the visitor will be an active participant in the "exhibition," which is a meditation on the meaning of objects valued by present members of the Museum "family" that accrue further meaning through a dialogue with the visitor.

I am thankful to cultural critic and professor Lewis Hyde, one of our nation's best thinkers on the artist in American culture, for his insightful essay for this catalog which ruminates on Emerson and Isabella Gardner's thinking.

The Museum is grateful to all who made the exhibition—and Lee Mingwei's residence—possible, in particular, Jennifer R. Gross, curator of contemporary art and public programs, for bringing leadership to the exhibition and residency; and Kristin Parker, public programs coordinator, for organizing Lee's work at the Museum. Special thanks also to Linda Graetz, director for school and teacher programs, and Janet Bertucci, school partnerships coordinator, for their commitment to realizing excellence in exhibition-related education programs. I also thank the teachers, administrators, and students from our neighborhood schools who participate in these programs.

Susan Sinclair, archivist; Patrick McMahon, the museum's former registrar and assistant to the curator of collections; and Isabelle Eaton, collections assistant, deserve special thanks for providing access to the archives and to the collection in support of artists during their residencies and *Eye of the Beholder* lecturers in preparing their materials. I also commend Chris Aldrich, who prepared the exhibition; and Ruth Abrahams, who designed the catalog. I also thank the Museum's Security staff, especially Felix Berrios, Hassan Bouhov, Jack Cashman, David Fisher, and Lyle Grindle, who made it possible for Lee Mingwei to move easily through the grounds and galleries.

The Museum's programs are enriched through the oversight and support of the Museum's Board Program Committee, chaired by Charles Wood, whose members include Sheryl Foti-Straus, Frieda Garcia, Kathryn O'Connell, Rob Radloff, Marcia Radosevich, David Scudder, and Jeanne Stanton.

To our funders, I am especially grateful. Public and artist programming at the Museum is made possible by the Barbara Lee Program Fund, the Lila Wallace–Reader's Digest Fund, and the National Endowment for the Arts. Major support for *Eye of the Beholder* programs has been provided by The Pew Charitable Trusts, the Stratford Foundation, The Boston Foundation, GTE, and the Clipper Ship Foundation.

A portion of the Museum's general operating funds for this fiscal year has also been provided through grants from the Institute of Museum and Library Services, a Federal agency; and the Massachusetts Cultural Council, a state agency that also receives support from the National Endowment for the Arts.

I am also grateful for the opportunity to collaborate with Susan Taylor, director, and Judy Fox, curator, of the Wellesley College Davis Museum and Cultural Center as they present an exhibition of past projects by Lee Mingwei concurrent with *The Living Room.*

Finally, I must thank the artist, Lee Mingwei, whose ideas, passions, and creative work bring meaning and joy to our lives.

Anne Hawley
Director

INTRODUCTION AND ACKNOWLEDGMENTS

Every work of art makes a long journey from imagination to realization, and many hands carry it on that journey. Even before the artist begins to dream, others have planted the seed in him. When Marion Stroud of Philadelphia's marvelous Fabric Workshop and Museum exhibited my *Letter Writing Project,* she not only generously underwrote the fabrication of the third writing booth but also introduced my work to Jennifer Gross of the Isabella Stewart Gardner Museum. Ms. Gross, having first encountered my work at the Whitney Museum of American Art, then invited me to be an artist in residence at the Gardner, with the support of the Museum's director, Anne Hawley. My month at the Gardner was enriched by the kind efforts of Jennifer and of Kristin Parker, public programs coordinator, who facilitated my exploration of Boston on preparator Chris Aldrich's bike (and on my own roller blades) and my daily swim at the Y. I think they realized early on that exercise would keep me alert and creative, and I thank them for not encouraging me to hole up in the Gardner's lovely old carriage house and struggle with ideas. I would also add that, without their exquisite taste and sensibility, *The Living Room* would not have fit so seamlessly into the Gardner's special ambience. Lewis Hyde's inspired and inspiring writing has influenced all my work, and it is good to have the chance to say so in print. My first encounter with his work was through a pirated Chinese translation of *The Gift* that I discovered fourteen years ago in Taiwan, and having his contribution in this catalogue is an overwhelming honor. Finally, I would like to express my utmost gratitude to Gregg Richardson and my family for their many years of support, challenge, and acceptance.

Lee Mingwei

OSMOSIS

Opportunities for creative participation are rarely offered to visitors of a museum's galleries, and the affirmation of the viewer's experience as the imbuing source of the art object's contemporary life is consistently absent in most museum and classroom introductions to art history. The viewer is more likely to be invited to look, read, and listen his or her way into the art on display through the digestion of didactic information presented through a concise wall label, audio tour, or docent. These sources deliver narratives that primarily seek to develop the visitor's knowledge of the historical context of an object or building but rarely acknowledge or challenge viewers to step up and share their insights into the artwork or think of themselves as contributors to the art-making process. The artist Lee Mingwei shares Isabella Stewart Gardner's understanding of this learned limit to art experience.

Isabella Stewart Gardner was familiar with and disliked the traditions of art education and museum display that were being established during her lifetime. Fenway Court was conceived and built in direct defiance of the austere display of art that encouraged laissez-faire aesthetic engagement on the part of the visitor. And although Mrs. Gardner never permitted the handling of objects in her Museum, she presented these items in a manner intent upon overwhelming and jumbling the senses as well as defying popular methods of aesthetic connoisseurship and morphological categorization.

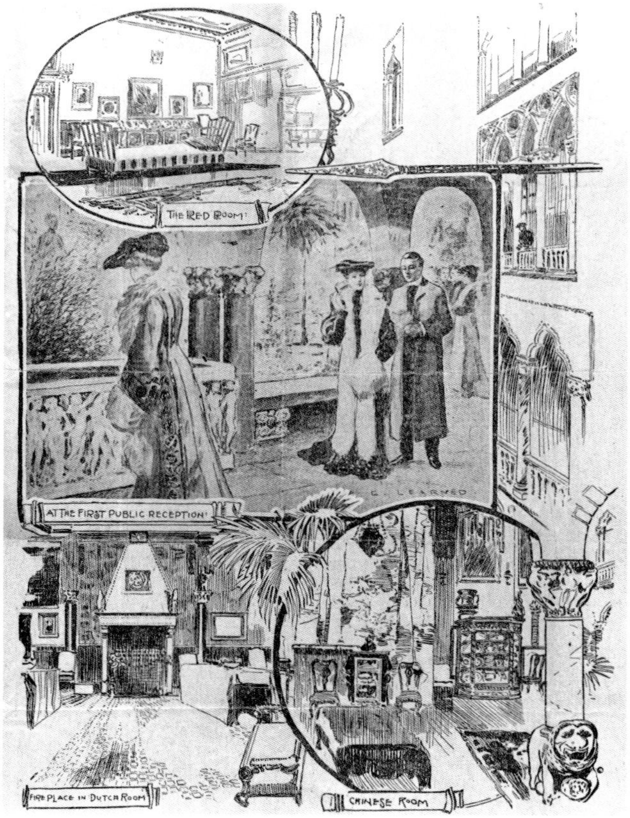

News clipping from the *Boston Herald*, February 24, 1903, regarding the Museum's opening night.

Isabella Gardner appreciated the value of an intellectual pursuit of knowledge pertaining to art; she had, in fact, apprenticed herself to Charles Eliot Norton and Bernard Berenson for that very purpose at the beginning of her own aesthetic journey. Yet she also believed the avenue of the mind comprised the less scenic segment of her own lifelong pilgrimage in pursuit of transformative experiences of beauty, pleasure, and enlightenment. After all, art and aesthetic experience made the woman. Gardner's life, until she had submitted herself to the vagaries of her aesthetic fancy, had been quite unremarkable for an upper-class Victorian woman. Her development into a cultural patron did not occur through reading books in Back Bay Boston but came about in increments inspired by a succession of aesthetic exposures. It began after she and Jack Gardner had taken to the road and discovered the great art collections of Europe and the ritualistically performative cultures and architectural environments of the East. Years later, this conversion found its ultimate realization as she attended to laying with her own hands the stones and the settings of her creative jewel, Fenway Court. Experience taught Isabella Gardner that if an individual could perpetually steep his or her modern sensibilities in a bath of unfamiliar beauty and celebration, the individual would see his or her own life anew and be revived, invigorated, and readied for the assaults of human existence. Creating the potential for physical and psychological immersion was a primary factor in her decision not to place labels or artificial lighting in the galleries at Fenway Court. She wanted the visitors to her Museum to feel their way into the tactile and sensual experience yielded up by her collection of rough stones, shimmering silk, shifting sunlight, and luminous images.

Before the mandate of Gardner's will, which stated that nothing in the galleries be added or deleted from the Museum's holdings, was effected, she continually reinstalled the galleries. Thereby she created new relationships between objects, a practice that refreshed her view of the collection and that of acquaintances who regularly visited the Museum. She also staged events through which her collection was to be experienced: poetry readings, dramas, concerts, bazaars, masses, tea ceremonies, and dinner parties. These choreographed exchanges between herself, her guests, and her collection infused the Museum and its audiences with a living energy.

A kindred desire to set a stage for others to engage in a fresh view of the world is at the core of the artistic practice of Lee Mingwei: "[I] psychologically or physically build a platform for people to come in and put their story and their experience in my context in their own language."[1] His artwork consists in making opportunities for focus and exchange, around an event or activity, for the types of interaction that he has observed on street corners, in cafés, in bookstores, and in churches. Like Isabella Gardner, he is an aesthetic facilitator more than an object maker, and like many artists of his generation, he is not so confident of the modern viewer's ability to be moved or even engaged by the mere presentation of an aesthetic object. Instead, he seeks to draw the viewer into an exchange that will slow him or her down and set in motion a personal involvement. Whether it is the admiration of an object, the writing of a letter to a friend or loved one, or making time for a conversation that is staged by Lee's projects, the viewer confirms what he or she believes is important in the world through his or her participation. Lee asks visitors to pause and reflect on what objects and thoughts they value and make beautiful through their recognition. In the title of a work Lee made in 1993, he clearly states his view of life and art, *Existence Depends on Your Attention.*

For Lee the human ability to choose is a divine power and beautiful. It is in choice that we are able to flex our individuality, as we decide what is worthy of the focus of our minds and energies in everyday life. Lee Mingwei believes this power of determination is as significant as life, and art, can become. His goal as an artist is to create an opportunity for those who encounter his work to recommit their lives to a mission of thought-filled, beautiful living, to provoke the all-important second glance. Isabella Stewart Gardner pursued this goal also, in the founding of her Museum.

Faith is an essential motivator in Lee's artistic gambit. His belief is more secular than religious, despite his training and practice as a Buddhist. For him, an exchange of energy, human to object, human to human, history to present, and present to future, is the elemental force that is the common basis of all life. This movement of molecules of matter, air, and water between elemental bodies perpetuates existence. For the formidable, forbidding human mind, the rediscovery of this fundamental pursuit can be transformative. Art is anything that effects such an exchange.

Born in 1964, Lee spent his childhood in Taiwan. At the age of eight, his parents began sending him to a Buddhist monastery each summer, where he learned from his master to see significance in everyday work. Lee attended a Benedictine high school in northern California and went on to study many areas of interest—biology, architecture, sculpture, textiles—before earning a B.F.A. from the California College of Arts and Crafts (CCAC), with honors in textile design, and then an M.F.A. from Yale University in sculpture.

While at CCAC, Lee studied with Suzanne Lacy, a feminist performance artist and activist well known for large-scale, theatrical performance pieces that illuminate social injustice and that often involve as collaborators those who are affected by that injustice. Lacy, in turn, had been strongly influenced by Allan Kaprow, with whom she had studied at Cal Arts. Kaprow is recognized as the influential creator of an early form of performance art developed in America in the late 1950s known as Happenings. These avant-garde performances usually required the participation of the audience in scripted but random events involving commonplace actions and materials. By scripting the audiences' participation and physically involving them in his artwork, Kaprow learned to envelop the viewer in actions that functioned as both metaphor and reality. Through his radical repositioning of the viewer inside the artwork, Kaprow shifted the location of aesthetic meaning from the privileged experience of the artist into the common experience of the viewer.

Kaprow published many of his reflections on artistic practice. In 1965 he wrote six Untitled Guidelines for Happenings. Excerpts from these guidelines (in italics below) read as the standards that lead Lee Mingwei's artistic practice:

> *—The line between art and life should be kept as fluid, and perhaps indistinct, as possible.*
>
> *—Therefore, the source of themes, materials, actions, and the relationships between them are to be derived from any place or period except from the arts, their derivatives, and their milieu. . . . Thus it is not that the known arts are "bad" that causes me to say "Don't go near them"; it is that they contain highly sophisticated habits. By avoiding the*

1. Mingwei Lee, "Interview with Mingwei Lee," *Ninety/Art in the Nineties* 29 (fall 1998): 68.

artistic modes there is the good chance that a new language will develop that has its own standards.

—It follows that audiences should be eliminated entirely. All the elements—people, space, the particular materials and character of the environment, time—can in this way be integrated. And the last shred of theatrical convention disappears. . . .

—Finally, there is this additional exception to the rule. A Happening may be scored for just watching. Persons will do nothing else. They will watch things, each other, possibly actions not performed by themselves, such as a bus stopping to pick up commuters. This would not take place in a theater or arena, but anywhere else. It could be an extremely meditative occupation when done devotedly; just "cute" when done indifferently. In a more physical mood, the idea of called-for watching could be contrasted with periods of action. Both normal tendencies to observe and act would now be engaged in a responsible way. At those moments of relative quiet the observer would hardly be a passive member of an audience; he would be closer to the role of a Greek chorus, without its specific meaning necessarily, but with its required place in the overall scheme. At other moments the active and observing roles would be exchanged, so that by reciprocation the whole meaning of watching would be altered, away from something like spoon-feeding, toward something purposive, possibly intense.[2]

Like Kaprow's Happenings, Lee's work is strongly rooted in an understanding of the importance of breaking down the boundaries that exist between art and life. Lee addresses this issue by focusing his energy on enabling acts of exchange in order to catalyze the viewer's active engagement in art making rather than through theatrical performance, which was Kaprow's primary medium. Lee's ability to achieve a transitive effect is not dependent on optical engagement alone, but embraces aural, tactile, oral, imaginative, and memory sensibilities. Art, food, service, conversation, and beauty have been the currency for these exchanges. Lee has found that these objects and acts ease the transmission or exchange of more intimate transactions involving systems of valuation, knowledge, experience, and faith.

2. Allan Kaprow, Untitled Guidelines for Happenings in *Theories and Documents of Contemporary Art*, Kristine Stiles and Peter Selz, eds. (Berkeley, Calif.: University of California Press, 1996), 709–14.

Lee's interest in diffusing and receiving faith, wonderment, and experience in life, as elemental realities of living, is partly the legacy of his undergraduate training in biology. His knowledge from this course of study of the interlocking, interdependence of cells in the creation of all life forms has stayed with him throughout his artistic training. His understanding of these systems led Lee to see humanity as a life-generating organism hindered by the limits of consciousness and afforded him the knowledge that if he was to be effective as an artist, his work must permeate that membrane. He came to the realization that his artistic medium would embrace methods of exchange, or osmosis, as it is identified in biology. His practice would become the creation and facilitation of situations that could break through the membrane of ego, that inflexible crust of self-consciousness and knowledge that molds human behavior in the face of external reality. These activities would enable the water of faith to disperse, diffuse, and to osmose the participant, the artist, and anyone else who willingly stepped into the arena of this exchange.

Aesthetics by Osmosis—the perfect introductory art history course title, perhaps? A pleasant alternative to those late-night, undergraduate, slide-memorization sessions with their blurring tide of images baked into the collective cerebral cortex with tongue-numbing quantities of caffeine, exhaustion-distorted top-forty tunes, and the dully solicitous voice of a not-to-be-remembered classmate repeating, "That's right. You're close . . . just a century off. Rhymes with. . . ." From this flash-card databank in deep storage, the subconscious teases out its visual shorthand of art knowledge: flash—naked girl on the half shell with stringy hair, think *vermicelli*, remember *Botticelli*; flash—man belly-up in Boston harbor floundering at the bow of a small boat in the grasp of a large, enraged fish, think *coping* with the fear of the shark, remember John Singleton *Copley*. "I loved that French artist, that one who painted a lot of blurry flowers, whose works were shown last year at the MFA, "focus on *blur* . . . think *Impressionist*, remember *Manet* . . . not quite right, think harder remember . . . *Monet*.

This identification game is familiar to any art enthusiast. We are commonly taught to learn art by rote. Perhaps this is why its practice and meanings retain such complex and conflicted auras in much of Western culture. Our tactile, subjective experience of many art objects seems untrustworthy because these insights and responses often seem ordinary or unrefined, and it is difficult for us to believe that art has been made for our enjoyment, our living with it in the present. In an age with few cultural patrons, we are hardwired to desire intellectual and aesthetic patronage over active, cultural engagement. Certainly we value art for its ability to record history, and for its beauty, but do we really believe that it is in these qualities alone that its ability to perpetually captivate and confound us lies? If this were so, would we not also covet our traditions of storytelling with equal intensity? Aesthetic engagement does more than confirm taste and preserve the past, it brings us pleasure and unsettles our subconscious. Great art, and even just good art, has the power to change how we see the world and how we stand in relationship to our lives.

Lee Mingwei hopes to infiltrate the viewer's life through the process of osmosis, which is defined in basic biology as the movement (diffusion) of water through a semipermeable membrane, from a region of higher concentration to a region of lower concentration. Osmosis is also known as the unconscious process of assimilation or absorption that resembles this diffusion. In Lee's experience, faith is the water, and consciousness (culture, tradition, and experience) is the membrane in the viewer, participant, and himself. The cell membrane, or human consciousness, is the outer living layer of beliefs through which the viewer structures his or her interface with life experiences. It is the reliance on these firmly held ideas about art and public interaction that he or she must give up in order to enter the dialogue of Lee's work. There is a need on the part of both project participants, those who choose to engage in the work rather than merely observe it, and visitors to be vulnerable and focused in their encounter with Lee's art in order to enter into this dialogue. The cell membrane is semipermeable and controls the passage of dissolved substances, or in this case, aesthetic experience, in and out of the cell. Many small particles are able to pass through it. Larger molecules, such as art history and connoisseurship, cannot pass through unless they have been digested and reduced in size and complexity. The movement of materials across the cell membrane into or out of the cell is called *transport*. In general, two types of transport exist: passive and active. In *passive transport*, the cell does not contribute energy for the movement of molecules across the membrane. Molecules move from an area of greater concentration to an area of lesser concentration by *diffusion*. This passive exchange takes place when the visitor first encounters Lee Mingwei's work and is open to considering one of his projects as art. *Active transport* occurs when the now-more-confident participant shares his or her experience with others.

Lee is often taken aback when people ask him what it is that he wants to tell the world through his art. He is more interested in what others say or can tell him about the world. The vitality of the exchange he experiences through his own work is his life. Lee knows his work has been effective when it has achieved what is called in biological terms an *isotonic solution*. An isotonic solution exists when the concentration of a dissolved substance on the outside of a cell is the same as the concentration of the dissolved substance inside the cell. In art, this is when the flow of experience from the viewer back through the work to the artist is equal to that of the flow from the artist out to the viewer. When the viewer's experience changes Lee's understanding of his own project and its sources in his life, moving him to a new place in the world, he knows the cycle has been completed. This is the basic biology of his art.

Lee Mingwei created his first interactive artwork, *Money for Art,* in 1994, shortly after leaving CCAC. Through photographic documentation, *Money for Art* tracks the life cycle of nine small sculptures the artist made in a café by folding ten-dollar bills. By undertaking his sculptural practice in a public space, Lee attracted the interest and response of strangers. Making sculpture was a significant component of Lee's work during this period, and his discovery of art as a currency of exchange through this project marked a significant shift in his practice as an artist from private to public. He realized that, more than the forms themselves, his willingness to share these objects created a universal language . If a person stopped to inquire after his work, Lee offered to give them a sculpture in exchange for receiving their commitment to stay in touch with him regarding the fate of the sculpture. The participants included Jennifer, a waitress; John, who was homeless and unemployed; Kan, a student; Sophia, a housewife; and a programmer, Tony. Lee photographed the life of the sculptures over the year. At the end of the year, Lee photographically documented the five remaining sculptures, the consumer goods (such as ice cream and a pair of shoes) for which three sculptures had been exchanged, and the absence of one sculpture, which had been stolen.

Following *Money for Art,* Lee engaged his viewers and himself in a much more subjective ritual. In 1995, *100 Days with Lily* documented Lee's relationship with a lily bulb that he planted, nurtured to maturity, and carried everywhere with him until after it had died. The artist photo-documented the life cycle of the lily and his relationship with it, overlaying the five images of its life cycle with a series of verbs that chronicled his daily interactions with the lily and the times at which they occurred: "day 1, 10:23, planting Lily; day 2, 06:34, sleeping with Lily; day 3, 12:05, eating with Lily; day 5, 07:12, meditating with Lily," etc. Lily died on day 79 and was exhumed on day 100.

This work honored the life cycle of all creatures but was conceived by the artist in recognition of his sense of loss and loneliness following his grandmother's death. The lily simultaneously functioned as a representation of the life and death of his grandmother, while affirming its own existence as a living entity that was animated by, and in kind animated, the life of the artist and those whom he encountered throughout the time of the project. While the artist's relationship began with and ended with his acting upon the lily (i.e., planting and exhuming), their interim relationship was noted by a series of verbs that recognize shared experiences, such as *breathing, walking, drinking, eating,* and *sleeping*. Unlike the impersonal record of actions undertaken by minimalist artists such as Carl Andre and Robert Morris on materials in the late 1960s, Lee's documentation pinpoints the dates and times of his engagements with the lily. He did this in order to reinforce and record the transformative, animating power of the intimacy shared between himself and the plant. Lee's appearance in traditional Chinese attire, carrying the lily, attracted strangers to him and encouraged them to ask questions about his project. These questions created a platform for intimacy between Lee and those who were willing to engage him in conversation. In turn, they often would share with Lee personal accounts of loss and renewal in their lives.

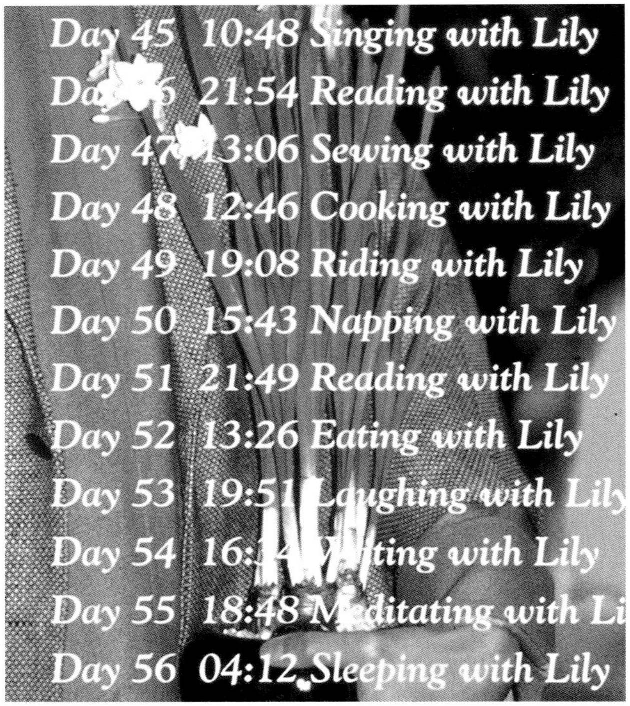

100 Days with Lily (detail), 1995, silver dye bleach print (Ilfochrome). Courtesy of Lombard/Freid Fine Art, New York, New York.

The Dining Project originated during Lee's first year as a graduate student in the M.F.A. program at Yale University, in 1995. Motivated by a desire to get to know people in his new community, Lee distributed flyers around campus inviting thirty participants to dine one-on-one with him in his studio. Lee's actions were inspired by his fond recollection of the personal and enlightening exchanges that took place around meals during his childhood. Of this work he has stated, "I was using the food as a medium for comfort, for introspection, for communication, for the germination of a relationship." The project was successful, as the artist made new friends, learned more about New Haven, and was encouraged to further explore issues raised by this type of art forum. To this day he has maintained many of the friendships that grew out of these first *Dining Project* meals.

The Dining Project was again presented in a one-person exhibition entitled "InteractExchange" at Lombard/Freid Fine Arts in New York in 1997. *The Dining Project* took place at night, after the gallery had closed to the public. The artist selected dining partners from a lottery and, several times a week, would prepare an Asian meal and serve it to one of them in the gallery space. In *The Dining Project*, the diners sat at a modified version of a Chinese dining platform filled with dried beans. Their feet rested on mounds of dry white rice. Menu items included Chinese cabbage, noodles with sesame paste, cubes of homemade tofu, and a bamboo platter piled with sweet, bean-filled buns. Lee continued to be interested and amazed by the dialogue that arose between himself and strangers when facilitated by food acting as a catalyst. The following day their recorded conversation was played back in the gallery, slightly altered (sped up or slowed down) and barely audible, as a testimony to the previous evening's activity.

A new version of *Money for Art* was also presented in this exhibition. Lee made origami sculptures from dollar bills and placed them on the shelves of two modular, wall-mounted shelving units. Visitors to the gallery were invited to take one of the origami pieces in exchange for a personal effect of equal value and to fill out a card stating their name and profession. A sample of the items that appeared on the shelves at the show included: a drawing, a prescription bottle, an engraved business card case, a bra, a takeout coffee cup, and an ATM card, along with its PIN number, due to expire that night. Since galleries are places where money is regularly exchanged for art, this piece was particularly well suited for exhibition in this commercial venue. As with the first version of the work, the participant and viewer were provoked to consider what constituted the art in the project—the sculpture, the objects left in exchange for the sculpture, or the act of exchange itself.

An exhibition in 1998 entitled "Way Stations," at the Whitney Museum of American Art in New York, also included *The Dining Project* as well as a new work, *The Letter Writing Project*. Both projects used familiar rituals as their primary medium. Inspired by Buddhist ritual and language, Lee regards these projects as "way stations," places of rest and renewal along the path of life. While *The Dining Project* was carried out much as it had been in 1997, *The Letter Writing Project* took place while the museum was open. Lee provided stationery and intimate writing enclosures in which he invited visitors to write letters to people living or dead, "the letters we have always intended to write but have put off with excuses." This project was also inspired by his grandmother's death and the artist's desire to maintain an intimate exchange with her through correspondence.

Lee asked visitors to write about an event in their life that had led them to one of three guiding principles: gratitude, insight, or forgiveness (a desire to either request or offer it), an event for which we would ask forgiveness. Lee reaffirmed these spiritual and emotional postures by providing three booths that offered three different positions in which the visitor could write, positions which corresponded to the three postures of meditation in Ch'an Buddhism (the Chinese ancestor of Zen): standing, sitting, and kneeling.

The visitor could choose whether the letters and addressed envelopes were clipped inside the booths and left for others to read or sealed inside an envelope and posted by the artist at the end of every week. The letters to the deceased were set aside to be burned at a later date in a river ceremony in emulation of a tradition in southeast Asia in which people build paper lanterns, write prayers on them, set them afire, then float them down a river. It is believed that the prayers will either rise up to heaven to the heavenly deities or descend into the water to the earthly deities.

The public response to *The Letter Writing Project* was staggering. At the end of the exhibition, Lee had collected more than nine thousand letters that had been written to the deceased and mailed countless pieces of correspondence to the living. He was

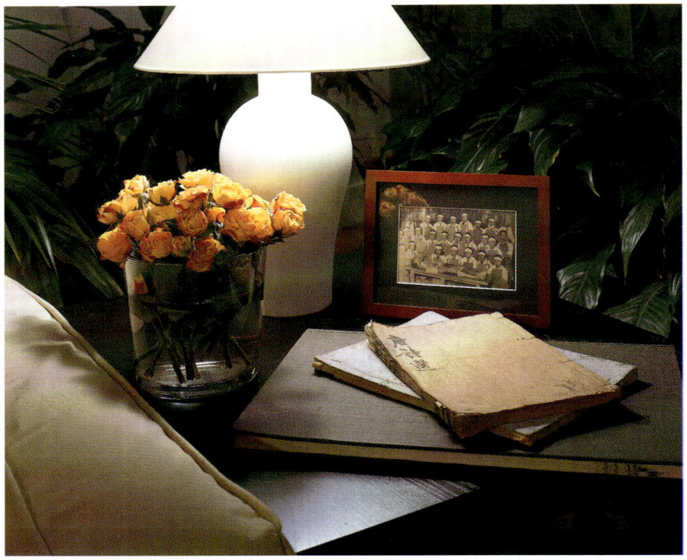

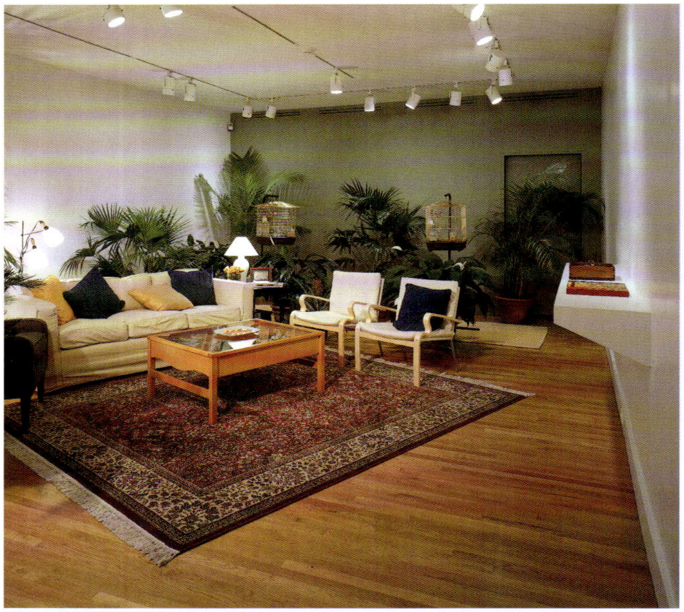

The Living Room (details), 2000, mixed media.

overwhelmed by many participants' willingness to share their vulnerabilities: openly weeping in the installation, sharing intimate accounts through conversation with others in the exhibition, and displaying envelopes for strangers to read that were addressed with painfully personal headings such as, "To my father which I will never see" or "In memory of Jamal." It appeared that *The Letter Writing Project* had facilitated a public healing ceremony by creating a setting in which the private act of writing became a public testimony.

Another aspect of *The Letter Writing Project* that came as a surprise to Lee—who had personally dined and folded his way through each of the exchanges that had taken place in his early work—was that the intimate exchanges occurring in this project did not rely on his personal presence as a catalyst. The visitors had desired and trusted the reciprocity of the project enough to participate merely on the basis of the invitation and opportunity. Lee had removed himself from the center of the arena and found that osmosis had naturally occurred without the direction of his hand once he had established a healthy environment for the essential catalyzing action of writing. Lee's absence also reinforced the presence and effect of less-active participants in the project. These secondary participants, or observers, who were not open to writing a letter themselves, happily read the correspondence of others and actively observed the contemplation and activity of the writing participants whose silhouettes could be seen through the translucent glass walls of the booths.

The opacity of the booths recalled lessons Lee had learned from an earlier work, entitled *Reflections* (1997), which was a free-standing booth made of muslin, divided into two chambers by a full-length, two-way mirror. Two participants completed the work. As they sat on either side of the mirror, each saw his or her reflection gradually merge with the face of the other. Their silhouettes could be seen by visitors through the translucent muslin walls. *Reflections* had been a means for Lee to test the membrane of perceptions that filter human experience: knowledge, memory, and imagination. The movement of one's own actions over the body of another challenged assumptions about interiority and exteriority in a shockingly invasive manner. The two-way mirror, or membrane, tested these boundaries by functioning simultaneously as a looking glass, a solid boundary, and a reflective/projective surface.

This membrane literally represented to the participants the inflexibility of their self-reflective view of the encounter. *Reflections* established that the primary physical relationship between participants was determined by a boundary, yet observers sensed this as well. As the membrane defined the relationship, it also functioned as a filter of the knowledge and cultural codes that it brought to the viewer's mind as he or she contemplated his or her counterpart at such close physical range. The movements of each participant's body over the body in reflection enabled them to observe their own habits and recognize them as a primary force in the establishment of their own identity.

In *The Letter Writing Project*, the booths with the written letters clipped to their frames also functioned literally as membranes for the exchange of grief and gratitude among Lee, the participants, and the observers. The participants readily projected their emotions onto something bigger or outside of themselves, and ultimately through the membrane of culture represented by the screen. Lee had successfully provided a platform for the type of communal exchange that has historically taken place in groups such as extended family units, churches, military affiliations, and social clubs, all of which had originally inspired his work. The desire for this forum of exchange proved to be more universal and profound than even Lee had imagined. For the artist, the physical exchange of salty tears was the one aspect of the project he had greatly underestimated, in that he had failed to provide tissues and a wastebasket to accommodate visitors' personal investment in his art. A project that had stemmed from the artist's desire to pay tribute to his grandmother in the end released emotions strong enough to transform both his conception of the project and the visitors and participants who encountered it in a public arena. The isotonic solution had been achieved, and Lee Mingwei's expectations, understanding, and life had been transformed by his art as much as by those he had set out to osmose.

As art critic Kay Larson has noted, writing a letter is a dialogue with oneself, as the intended recipient is not present but is constructed by the writer as a projection of his or her needs and expectations.[3] Lee Mingwei undertook *The Letter Writing Project* and *The Dining Project* as correspondences with many recipients: his family, his friends, his grandmother, and the public. Isabella Gardner undertook the creation of her Museum as a dialogue of a kindred spirit. In building Fenway Court and making it available to the public, she, like Lee, constructed a situation in which the beauty of the collection and her hospitality created an opportunity for the transference of energy. Through pleasure, Gardner sought to control and shift the visitors' frame of reference in order to shake them out of their unchallenged world-view. While the magnificence of Fenway Court has partially fulfilled Mrs. Gardner's mission, since her death there have been few opportunities for the daily visitor to be a recipient of her legacy of hospitality.

Lee Mingwei's *The Living Room* was conceived to recognize this disconnect between Mrs. Gardner's living Museum and the more static monuments encountered by the modern visitor. As the artist has written regarding this work: "The two concepts which are the basis for this project are hospitality and collection. Mrs. Gardner created this museum not only to house her treasured objects but also as a place for her to be generous and hospitable to her friends and the public. I want to offer museum visitors the hospitality which was once a part of this house, with staff, members, and others who are intimately connected to the museum taking on Mrs. Gardner's role as host in a specially created living room within the museum."[4]

The Living Room has been created to expand the one-on-one reciprocal exchange that already occurs in the Museum between guards and visitors, as well as among artists, educators, and children. Lee Mingwei sees these activities as a source of energy that makes the Museum function as a living organism on a day-to-day basis. Through his expansion of these organic processes of sharing and entertaining, Lee believes the Museum regains more of its original function as a catalyst for change rather than falling back on its function as a mausoleum for inanimate, exotic objects.

Lee's invitation to the Museum's staff, and others with longstanding intimate relationships with this collection, to act as hosts of *The Living Room* for two days includes bringing objects of either artistic importance or personal importance into *The Living Room* to

3. Kay Larson, "Transforming Death's Wound: A Healing Art," *The New York Times*, November 15, 1998.

4. Lee Mingwei in correspondance with curator Jennifer R. Gross during his residency at the Gardner Museum, June 1999.

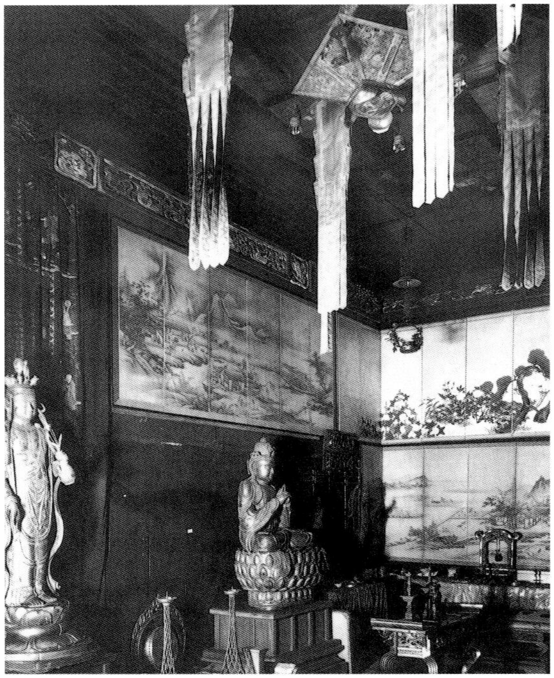

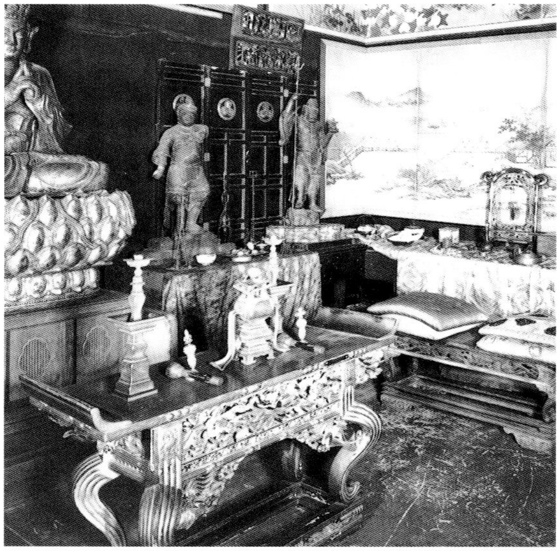

Chinese Room, west wall, north corner, and ceiling (at top) and north and west sections (above). Photographs by Joseph Pratt, 1961.

share with Museum visitors. The space is comfortably equipped, with modern furnishings, plants, and even songbirds, in order to offer visitors a welcoming place to rest on their journey through the collection. The host serves the visitor with refreshments as well as with a willingness to answer questions about the collection, Isabella Gardner, the objects the host has brought, or the host's personal experience of the Museum. The forty hosts were selected by lottery from a list of volunteers.

This project challenges the popular understanding of museum collections and their presentation as an impersonal confrontation with objects that have been removed from their native and historical context. Lee Mingwei conceived of *The Living Room* as a sanctuary from the modern experience of museums and modeled it (in function rather than design) after a traditional Japanese tearoom. Lee's consciousness of the need for an edited, intimate environment for a meaningful encounter with art and life at the Gardner Museum is rooted in the traditions of the Japanese tea ceremony, which derive from Chinese culture. The hosts of *The Living Room* function not only as surrogate Isabella Gardners but also as teahouse storytellers who during the Song Dynasty (960–1279) in China were popular counterparts of the troubadours in medieval Europe. In the Ming Dynasty (1368–1644), etiquette rigorously required that every caller regardless of rank or business be served tea upon his arrival, the traditional sign of Chinese hospitality. It is Lee's desire that all Museum visitors be welcomed into an experience of *The Living Room* in the spirit of the tearoom tradition.

Tea was known in Japan before the Kamakura era, (1185–1338), but its first wider propagation is generally ascribed to Eisai (1141– 1215), the Zen teacher who brought tea seeds from China and had them cultivated in his friend's monastery grounds.[5] In the practice of the Japanese tea ceremony, a sanctuary is created where one can take solace in the tranquility of the spirit. Chanoyu, which means "hot water for tea," is known in English as the tea ceremony and has as its objective a relaxed communion between the host and his or her guests. It is a composite form of art created by blending Chinese tea-drinking customs with elements of Zen philosophy. Chanoyu brings together the etiquette of serving tea, the aesthetic

5. Daisetz T. Suzuki, *Zen and Japanese Culture* (New York: Bollingen Series LXIV, Princeton University Press, 1959), 272.

contemplation of landscape gardens, tea utensils, paintings, and flower arrangement, and other elements that combine to exist in a harmonious and aesthetically pleasing ceremony whose ultimate aim is the attainment of deep spiritual satisfaction.

The link between Lee's Chinese heritage and the Museum's ties to Japan through the ritual of the tea ceremony have great significance at the Gardner Museum because of Isabella Gardner's own transformative relationship with Okakura Kakuzō, Japanese art critic, author, and educator.[6] Okakura first met Isabella Gardner in 1904, when he came to Boston to assume a post as adviser to the Asiatic Department at the Museum of Fine Arts. He came to know her following a letter of introduction the American artist John La Farge wrote to Mrs. Gardner in March of 1904:

> I suppose that it is merely a question of time that he [Okakura Kakuzō] should have many introductions to you. One of his purposes in Boston is to do something for the arrangement or catalogue of the collection in the Museum. You probably know as much about him as I do myself by reputation. But I should like to add to any knowledge you may have of him, my statement that he is the most intelligent critic of art, and I might almost say of everything, that I know of. His very great learning in certain ways is balanced by the perception of the uselessness of much that he knows. I think that he is one of the very few persons whom you should not miss enjoying, and he might also be of use to you in any question of detail of authenticity or anything similar.[7]

Okakura's effect on Isabella Gardner was significant, and she lauded his profound influence to friends. The distinct change he inspired in her character was also noted by longtime acquaintances.[8] Isabella's friendship with Okakura continued until his death, in 1913. Unlike Bernard Berenson, Okakura did not act as consultant to Mrs. Gardner for purchases for her collection, as most of the Museum's Asian collections were already installed, but he introduced her to ideas that invested her experience of art with new meaning.[9]

Okakura published *The Book of Tea* in 1906. In it, he revealed the aesthetic lessons chanoyu has to teach Western audiences. It is remarkable how much of his insight into Western culture at the turn of the century reads as apt commentary on aesthetic issues at the end of the century. Okakura spoke of chanoyu as a "religion of aestheticism" that trains the practitioner's eye to see the world around him or her without the distorting lens of social custom. While the utensils used in the tea ceremony are treasured and handled with great respect, they are ordinary objects that have been adapted for aesthetic use and appreciation, as have many of the objects in Isabella Gardner's Museum. So also are the objects Lee Mingwei encourages the hosts of *The Living Room* to bring in to the Museum to share with visitors. Hence, these objects are not to be judged against an ideal of formal beauty but against the standard of valuation by which the host chose them.

Lee realizes that this individual standard of assessment might challenge the aesthetic standards that have become synonymous

6. *The Living Room* also pays homage to the wonderful collection of Asian artifacts in the Buddhist meditation room treasured by Isabella Gardner during her lifetime that was dispersed in 1971.

7. Gardner Collection, Isabella Stewart Gardner Museum.

8. Mary Berenson, wife of Bernard Berenson, wrote of Isabella Gardner's declaration of Okakura's profound personal effect on Gardner's character in a letter to her family in January of 1914: "B.B. said to her [Mrs. Gardner] the last day that although he had found her fascinating and wonderful before, he had never loved her until this time, for she had never been lovable. She wept at this, and said it was true, and perhaps she would have gone to her grave with her hard heart and selfish character if it had not been for a Japanese mystic named Okakura, who was attached to the Boston Museum as expert. He was the first person, she said, who showed her how hateful she was, and from him she learnt her first lesson of seeking to love instead of to be loved. She admitted that many of her bad habits remained, but said that the core of herself was quite different, and she wanted to get rid of old evils. It was really touching. She is truly one of the most astonishing personalities we have ever known, and at last we really care for her as a human being" (from Mary Berenson, *Mary Berenson: A Self-Portrait from Her Letters and Diaries,* Barbara Strachey and Jayne Samuels, eds. [London: Victor Gollancz Ltd., 1983], 194).

9. The Gardners set off on a tour of the world in May of 1883 that began in Japan and continued on into China, through Indochina, including Angkor Wat, southeast Asia, India, Egypt, and on to Europe. They returned to the United States in the summer of 1884. They were inspired during their journey by a series of lectures given by Professor Edward Sylvester Morse at their home at 152 Beacon Street. Japan retained a continuing presence in the Gardners' lives upon their return to Boston. They built a Japanese garden featuring irises and stone lanterns at Greenhill and continued to build on the collection of Japanese artifacts that they had begun on their trip abroad. This foundation was greatly expanded by Isabella Gardner, after the death of Jack Gardner, as she completed the installation of Fenway Court. Her sources in Boston were two major dealers in Japanese and Chinese art, Matsuki Bunkio and the Yamanaka Company. She acquired numerous screens and sculptures from them which she used to enhance the atmosphere of the Museum.

with the Gardner Museum's identity but hopes that the questions this raises will broaden the aesthetic appreciation of each visitor as he or she is introduced to a new understanding of the value placed on these objects by each host. Ultimately, it is this newly won vision that Lee believes will be reapplied to the Museum's permanent collection, increasing its value beyond what Okakura described in *The Book of Tea* as the two primary plagues of art appreciation in modern times:

> 1) Our finite nature, the power of tradition and conventionality, as well as our hereditary instincts, [to] restrict the scope of our capacity for artistic enjoyment. Our very individuality establishes in one sense a limit to our understanding and our aesthetic personality seeks its own affinities in the creations of the past. It is true that with cultivation our sense of art appreciation broadens, and we become able to enjoy many hitherto unrecognized expressions of beauty. But, after all, we see only our own image in the universe—our particular idiosyncrasies dictate the mode of our perceptions.
>
> 2) It is much to be regretted that so much of the apparent enthusiasm for art at the present day has no foundation in real feeling. In this democratic age of ours men clamour for what is popularly considered the best, regardless of their feelings. They want the costly, not the refined; the fashionable, not the beautiful. To the masses, contemplation of illustrated periodicals, the worthy product of their own industrialism, would give more digestible food for artistic enjoyment than the early Italians or the Ashikaga masters, whom they pretend to admire. The name of the artist is more important to them than the quality of the work. As a Chinese critic complained many centuries ago, *People criticise a picture by their ear.* It is this lack of genuine appreciation that is responsible for the pseudo-classic horrors that to-day greet us wherever we turn.[10]

The Taoist theory of the all-containing involves the conception of a continued need of change in decorative motifs in order to throw off the limits of human nature. In *The Living Room* this is fulfilled by the continuous flow of objects brought into the gallery by the changing tide of hosts. In the traditional tearoom, the space is kept absolutely empty, except for what may be placed there temporarily to satisfy some aesthetic mood. Lee, however, chooses to maintain a modern setting infused with Isabella Gardner's spirit through plants and singing birds. In chanoyu, some special art object is brought in for the occasion, and everything else is selected and arranged to enhance the beauty of the principal theme. This focused aesthetic is vital to enabling the spirit of chanoyu, as it is believed that a real comprehension of the beautiful being is possible only through concentration upon one central motive, rather than many themes, much as one cannot listen to different pieces of music at the same time. This is in direct contrast to the profusion of sensations yielded up by Isabella's installation of the Museum, which saturates the visitor's senses in a riot of texture, color, sounds, and smells.[11]

Mrs. Gardner desired the visitor to her Museum to come with serious aesthetic intent and respect. She was wary of "gawkers" but was keenly interested in making available to individuals willing to adopt a posture of faith the opportunity to be overwhelmed with wonder and surprise by the many unanticipated incidents she staged in the galleries as well as by the activities that she hosted at the Museum. For Isabella Gardner, no boundaries existed between art and life. In Lee Mingwei's *The Living Room,* no such boundaries exist either. The visitor is invited into a process of aesthetic commerce that utilizes aesthetic enthusiasm, shared personal experience, and the pleasures availed by the Gardner Museum as its primary mediums of

10. Okakura Kakuzō, *The Book of Tea* (Japan: Kodansha International, Ltd., 1989), 102, 103.

11. Ibid., 102, 103. Okakura wrote of his distress in the face of this Western convention in *The Book of Tea* (ibid., 105): "Thus it will be seen that the system of decoration in our tea-rooms is opposed to that which obtains in the West, where the interior of a house is often converted into a museum. To a Japanese, accustomed to simplicity of ornamentation and frequent change of decorative method, a Western interior permanently filled with a vast array of pictures, statuary, and bric-a-brac gives the impression of mere vulgar display of riches. It calls for a mighty wealth of appreciation to enjoy the constant sight of even a masterpiece, and limitless indeed must be the capacity for artistic feeling in those who can exist day after day in the midst of such confusion of colour and form as is to be often seen in the houses of Europe and America." Okakura's commentary in this passage is uncanny in light of his familiarity with Gardner's project and their intimate exchange of aesthetic passions. His frank address of the marked cultural differences at the root of their spiritual and aesthetic faith confirms the singular nature of this relationship in Gardner's life and the deep mutual respect that was at the root of their friendship.

exchange in the sensual yet calm environment of *The Living Room*. It is in such a place, where contemporary experience is the enlivening force of exchange, that a focused inquiry into the issues raised by the interface of modern aesthetics with the historical treasures of the museum could be initiated. As Okakura wrote almost a century ago of the complementary relationship between contemporary and historical art, "Art, to be fully appreciated, must be true to contemporaneous life. It is not that we should ignore the claims of posterity, but that we should seek to enjoy the present more. It is not that we should disregard the creations of the past, but that we should try to assimilate them into our consciousness."[12] Lee Mingwei's *The Living Room* creates the opportunity for modern-day visitors to the Gardner Museum to engage in a dialogue between history and the present, Isabella Gardner and Okakura, as well as with each other. Such dialogue cannot help but transform both their expectations of art and Isabella Stewart Gardner's "permanent" collection. *Aesthetics by Osmosis* is open to anyone who is interested. For those willing to participate in its ebb and flow, art history may never look the same.

Jennifer R. Gross

12. Ibid, 86. Okakura wrote at length on the lack of regard for contemporary art in his own day. In *The Book of Tea* (104–5) his writings on the subject could be read as an apt address of art-funding debates currently raging in America: "The claims of contemporary art cannot be ignored in any vital scheme of life. The art of today is that which really belongs to us: it is our own reflection. In condemning it we but condemn ourselves. We say that the present age possesses no art—who is responsible for this? It is indeed a shame that despite all our rhapsodies about the ancients we pay so little attention to our own possibilities. Struggling artists, weary souls lingering in the shadow of cold disdain! In our self-centered century, what inspiration do we offer them? The past may well look with pity at the poverty of our civilisation; the future will laugh at the barrenness of our art. We are destroying art in destroying the beautiful in life. Would that some great wizard might from the stem of society shape a mighty harp whose strings would resound to the touch of genius."

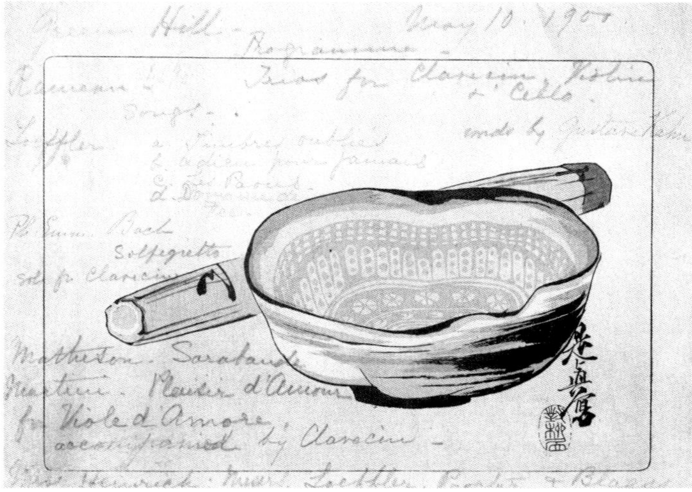

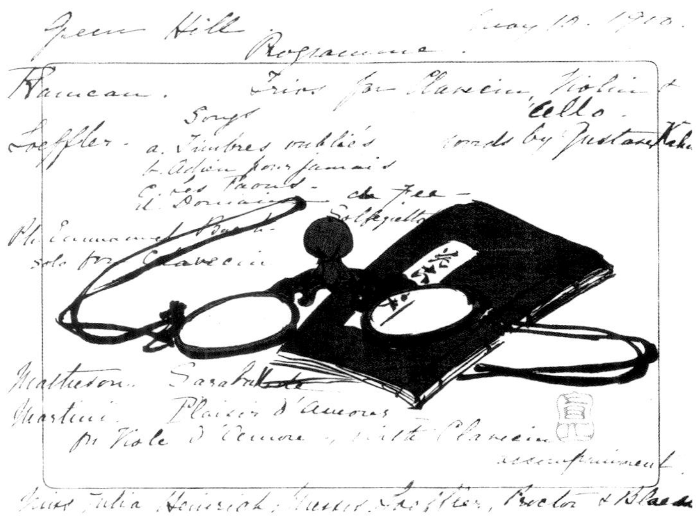

Music programs, handwritten by Mrs. Gardner. May 10, 1900, for a performance at Green Hill, her Brookline residence.

ISABELLA'S WILL

Not far from the Gardner Museum sits the Boston Common, site of an important moment in American spiritual life, for it was there that Ralph Waldo Emerson had the famous epiphany reported in the first chapter of his first book, *Nature* (1836): "Crossing a bare common, in snow puddles, at twilight, under a clouded sky, without having in my thoughts any occurrence of special good fortune, I have enjoyed a perfect exhilaration. I am glad to the brink of fear. . . . Standing on the bare ground,—my head bathed by the blithe air and uplifted into infinite space,—all mean egotism vanishes. I become a transparent eyeball; I am nothing; I see all; the currents of the Universal Being circulate through me; I am part or parcel of God."[1]

His "mean egotism" disappeared, he says, but I take it that egotism of some other sort remained, for these three sentences alone contain the word "I" six times. It is a solitary, individualist epiphany, an image of one consciousness being touched by the divine without apparent mediation of community or church.

Thus it is no accident, I think, that Emerson placed himself on the common, and a "bare" one at that, with snow puddles and clouds, for the common in America was imagined as the place where a "common man" or "common woman" might walk or where all who walked became "common" by their presence there. That is to say, the common in America was exactly not the commons

1. Ralph Waldo Emerson, *Nature, Addresses and Lectures* (Boston: Houghton Mifflin, 1921), 9–10.

of Europe. A common in America was a republican space where rich and poor could meet with equal privilege; the commons in Europe was an aristocratic space where rich and poor met and enacted their differences.

I will say more about what that means before I am done, but first let me come back to that near neighbor of the Boston Common, the Gardner Museum, for it is the Museum that has set me to thinking about the commons. Lee Mingwei's project at the Museum responds to Isabella Stewart Gardner's original enterprise, which was to create a space that was at once her private home (she lived on the fourth floor) and a building open "for the education and enjoyment of the public forever" (as her will declared). Now, a century after the Museum was chartered, Lee Mingwei offers us a chance to interrogate that original impulse and reimagine what it might mean. Why might you invite strangers into your home to see your art? Why might you turn your home into a public space? And what is a "public" space in this case? Is a museum like a common pasture where we, the public, come to graze on beauty? How far are we from the Boston Common, and how near?

For my answer I propose to offer a short reading of Mrs. Gardner's will, probated July 23, 1924, in the Suffolk County courthouse, for it is the will that sets the terms by which the Gardner Museum has operated for the last seventy-five years and will operate, if Mrs. Gardner has her way, "forever."

"I, Isabella Stewart Gardner . . . do make and publish this my last will." Thus does our text begin, and it is a beginning that we may do well to pause over. Isabella Stewart was born in New York in 1840; she married John Lowell Gardner in 1860 and moved to Boston. Both families were rich (the Stewarts: Irish linen, mining; the Gardners: sailing ships, the China trade, railroads, mines, mills), but more than that, they had a certain pride of ancestry, the Stewarts especially. A man named Morris Carter is named in the will as the first director of the Museum (and given the fourth floor apartment, a month's vacation, and two servants); he was also Mrs. Gardner's first biographer, and in his biography, he has this to say:

> Various genealogists assert that the Stewarts were descended from King Fergus I, a contemporary of Alexander the Great. Mrs. Gardner quite naturally had a cult for Mary Stuart and for the martyred Charles I. She possessed a few precious Stuart relics: fragments of silk and lace, said to be parts of dresses once worn by Mary Stuart. . . . The death of Charles of England, king and martyr, was occasionally—not regularly—commemorated at Fenway Court [as the Museum is called] by a little supper for a few enthusiasts, and an intimate, romantic service in the chapel.[2]

Some odd touches occur in that report—the genealogists "assert," the interest in Mary Stuart is "quite natural," the lace is "said to be" royal—that make one suppose the facts may have suffered a good admixture of fantasy. But whatever the true roots, we have the true fruit: this Isabella had a fondness for royalty. She was, above all, attracted to anything connected to royal Isabellas. The Museum collection contains images of, or materials associated with, Queen Isabella Católica of Spain, Isabella Clara Eugenia the Archduchess, Isabella of Portugal, and Isabella d'Este (whom Bernard Berenson called, as he urged a purchase upon his patron, "the greatest and most fascinating lady of the Renaissance—your worthy precursor and patron saint"[3]).

Mrs. Gardner was also very much interested in the Stuart kings. Ornaments throughout Fenway Court show the Scottish thistle and white rose. She was a member of the Order of the White Rose, a society inspired by Sir Walter Scott's romantic versions of history. When Berenson was persuading her to buy Titian's *Rape of Europa*, he reminded her that it had once been meant to be a gift to Charles I, a Stuart king, and had ended up in the collection of Lord Darnley, also a Stuart.[4] "It would be poetic justice," Berenson wrote, "that a picture once intended for a Stewart [sic] should at last rest in the hand of a Stewart."[5]

And, if we are trying to imagine what it means to offer the paintings in Fenway Court to "the public forever," then we should pause to wonder what it means that the death of Charles I was remembered in that space. In *Walden*, Henry Thoreau says that the newspapers mostly have no news to report; to his mind, the last bit of real news was dated 1649—the year that Cromwell and the

2. Morris Carter, *Isabella Stewart Gardner and Fenway Court* (Boston: Houghton Mifflin, 1925), 3–4.
3. Bernard Berenson as quoted in ibid., 109.
4. Ibid., 157.
5. Bernard Berenson as quoted in ibid., 158.

Puritans beheaded Charles I. That is to say, for some Americans the death of Charles I began the movement that led to the Great Republic and its experiment in democracy.

It seems odd at first, then, to find someone born a generation after Thoreau mourning the death of that hapless seventeenth-century monarch. It is less odd if one revisits the changes that American civic culture underwent in the late nineteenth century. To give too brief a summary of a complicated history: before the American Civil War, the rhetoric of "the Great Republic" held public displays of wealth and class in check; after the Civil War, that rhetoric lost its power, and the rich came forward, much at ease displaying themselves as not just rich, but deservedly so, naturally so.

That change is well reflected in the emergence of the country's elite cultural institutions. The years between 1870 and 1890 brought the creation of the Metropolitan Museum of Art, the Boston Museum of Fine Arts, the Art Institute of Chicago, the Boston Symphony Orchestra, the Metropolitan Opera Association, the Detroit Institute of Arts, the Cincinnati Museum of Art, the Chicago Symphony Orchestra, and more. On the whole, these institutions were all created privately. Their styles and programs reflected, and offered "to the public," the tastes of America's financial and social elites.[6] Mrs. Gardner's Fenway Court belongs to their era. Perhaps it was the greater privacy (she was the Museum's sole benefactor) that allowed her to be more direct and—what word? playful? confrontational?—in appropriating royalist trappings to present her work to Puritan Boston.

If we come back to the will and move beyond "Isabella Stewart," we find the late Mrs. Gardner giving a lot of money to worthy causes, relatives, and friends ("to Pablo Casals, I give my violincello [sic] now in his possession"), after which she names seven people, all men, to be the trustees of the Museum. She establishes a fund for its operation ($1,200,000), and she lays down a number of constraints under which the Museum must operate.

She says, for example, that the director "shall . . . charge and collect a fee from visitors to the Museum, as in my opinion the greatest good to the public and the community will be attained by charging such fee." She says, "I believe that the interest in the Museum and its value to the public will best be sustained and furthered by opening it only on certain days and also by charging an admission fee."

Before Mrs. Gardner's death, the Museum was open to the public, but not regularly. In 1903, the first year the public were admitted, the entrance fee was one dollar. I have had a look at the *Statistical Abstract of the United States* for the year 1904 and find there that, if you were importing goods into the United States, one dollar would buy thirty pounds of herring, forty pounds of rice, seventeen gallons of wine, eleven pounds of coffee, or six pounds of tea. Multiply any of those by current prices, and you will see that a 1903 dollar was not an insignificant sum. To open the Museum "only on certain days" and to charge such a fee means that, if Mrs. Gardner's original Museum was a commons, it was a gated—or stinted, to employ a British term—commons.

That is what the commons were in England under the Stuart kings, and before. The commons in premodern England were *not* like American public parks or the Boston Common—open more or less freely to all who might want to use them. They were highly stinted, meaning that while by custom commoners had a set of use rights in the common, the use rights had clear limits. A village family might, for example, have the right to let their cattle graze on the common, but only during one part of the year and only so many cattle as they could maintain on their own land during the rest of the year. Or they might have the right to cut rushes on the common, but only between Christmas and Candlemas. Or they might have the right to cut the branches of trees on the common, but only up to a certain height and only after November 10. Or they might have the right to cut furze—a thorny, evergreen shrub—but only so much as can be carried on one's back and only to heat one's own house.[7]

Not only were rights in common stinted, they brought obligations with them. Under the manorial system in medieval England, for example, commoners had to help the lord of the manor plough his fields and reap his crop; they had to maintain his hedges; they had to bring him honey, eggs, and chickens; and so forth. On the

6. I am indebted to Neil Harris for this list and to his 1995 lecture to Grantmakers in the Arts, "Public Subsidies and American Art."

7. See E. P. Thompson, *Customs in Common* (New York: New Press, 1993), 132, 142, 147; and Susan Cox, "No Tragedy in the Commons," *Environmental Ethics* 7 (spring 1985): 54.

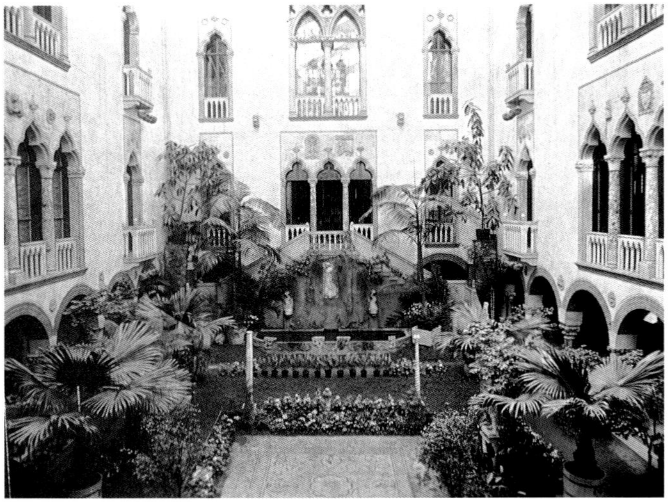

Courtyard of the Isabella Stewart Gardner Museum, 1908.
Photograph by Thomas Marr.

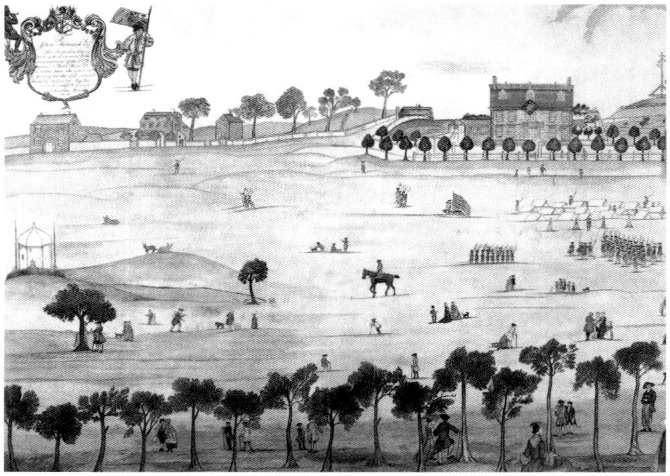

A *Perspective View of Part of the Commons,* engraved by Sidney L. Smith, 1902 after a watercolor by Christian Remick in 1768. Courtesy of the Boston Athenaeum.

other hand, the lord's rights were also stinted; above all, he could not abridge the use rights held by commoners. His land was not wholly his; it was, rather, a place for staging the mutual duties of premodern aristocracy.

So, what kind of space was Mrs. Gardner's Museum in 1903? If she charged one dollar at the door and opened it only "certain days," it was not a public commons but, at best, a gated one. On the other hand, when it was open, the gate was pure money, meaning that there was none of the reciprocal rights and duties that marked a manorial commons. Neither feudal nor republican, it was at best some strange hybrid of the two, a point I shall return to when we have finished with our reading of the will.

The fee and the limited hours are the least of the constraints Mrs. Gardner suggests for her Museum. Here is the document's key clause: "If at any time the Trustees . . . shall place for exhibition in the Museum . . . any pictures or works of art other than such as I or [the Museum] own . . . , or if they shall at any time change the general disposition or arrangement of any articles . . . , then I give the said land, Museum, pictures, [etcetera] . . . , to the President and Fellows of Harvard College, in trust to sell." That is to say, the will stipulates that nothing may be added to the collection, nothing may be sold, and nothing may be moved—or else.

A "last will" embodies a unique action, an action after the death of the actor. And there must be two sorts of "last wills": those that emphasize the "last" and those that emphasize the "will." The former give in order to give up. They announce a bequest—ten thousand dollars to Aunt Harriet—and that's the end of it. Aunt Harriet is now the actor, and she may burn the money, or buy hats, or invest in sensible bonds. Isabella Stewart Gardner's will is not much about giving up. She makes a few outright bequests, yes, but she also demands that a memorial mass be said annually on her birthday in the little chapel on the third floor of Fenway Court, and more to the point, she demands that her Museum stay as it was on the day she died. You may not like the way she hung that Rembrandt self-portrait, but if you move it, the lawyers from Harvard will show up with appraisers from Sotheby's in tow.

What does it mean, this constraint of all change, this freezing of the space?

I wonder, first of all, if the controlling impulse doesn't have to do with those seven men appointed to be trustees. Mrs. Gardner wants it clear that they are there to guard her creation, not to revise it. The Gardner is what is called a "house museum," and in this case, a *woman's* house, especially (Mrs. Gardner did not begin to build Fenway Court until her husband had died). The building, its contents, and its interior arrangement are her work of art. During her lifetime, her will, her agency, was in the architecture, the purchases, the arrangement, the lighting, and so forth. Each room is a kind of painting with paintings. We would rightly protest if someone rearranged a collage by Picasso; Mrs. Gardner's will protests in advance any attempt to rearrange the collage of Fenway Court.

We have, then, a woman suspicious of what the men will do when left alone but, nonetheless, obliged to turn the house keys over to them—which is to say, Mrs. Gardner may have anticipated tension between her work and the men she left to oversee it, but she was not a feminist in the modern style. She took no real interest in two of the defining political movements of her lifetime, the abolition of slavery and the fight for woman's suffrage. She was a Victorian with a royalist sensibility and private money. If we are looking for a nineteenth-century image of woman's power to match with Mrs. Gardner, we should probably go to Queen Victoria herself, rather than to any suffragette. The motto of Mrs. Gardner's Museum is *"c'est mon plaisir,"* which means not only "it is my pleasure," but also "it is my will"; and her "last will" spells out the regal pleasure of an American aristocrat interested in preserving her own image on her own terms.

Mrs. Gardner had a long-standing and somewhat theatrical concern with how she was seen, and when. At the time that Fenway Court was built, she had a tablet placed over the main entrance inscribed, "The Isabella Stewart Gardner Museum in the Fenway MDCCCC," but she immediately covered this with a marble slab. The cover came off when she died.[8] Similarly, John Singer Sargent's famous 1888 painting of Mrs. Gardner, depicting her as a sensuous goddess complete with Renaissance halo, was off-limits to the public until she died. It sits in the Gothic room on the third floor of the Museum so that, with her death, "the public" gets to travel through the house museum, room after room, until—having finally come to the little chapel where her birth is celebrated every April 14—one enters the final room to find the creator herself revealed.

Mrs. Gardner managed, then, to have her death prompt a new revelation of both her name and image. But this concern with how and when her creations were seen was a part of her style during her lifetime as well. There is a striking story about the 1902 preparations for the opening of Fenway Court. At that time the building contained a magnificent, high-ceilinged music room. Mrs. Gardner wanted to test the acoustics of the room with a live audience, but she also did not want anyone to see it before the opening. What to do? She invited for a concert at Fenway Court an audience of children from the Perkins Institution for the Blind.[9]

Beyond the breathtaking sense that the world and its inhabitants were there for her use, we have here an earlier version of the will's marked concern that her work be seen on her terms or not at all. Nor was the opening of Fenway Court the first time she had displayed her will in that regard. Mrs. Gardner had lived in a house at 152 Beacon Street in Boston before she moved to Fenway Court in 1904. Before she sold the Beacon Street house, she had all the interior woodwork and fireplaces removed, installing them wherever possible in her apartment at Fenway Court. Moreover, the new owner of 152 Beacon Street got possession of the house only on condition that he tear it down, build a new one, and change the number to 150. As Morris Carter remarks, "Thus Mrs. Gardner, who craved continuity and the perpetuation of her personality, transported to the new location whatever intimate association she could and obliterated what must be left behind."[10]

Mrs. Gardner's will offers the trustees the same options when it comes to the Museum: perpetuation or obliteration. Her creation must remain solidly in the condition she left it, or it must be liquefied—"convert[ed] . . . into money," the will says, and the money given away. If it works as she wanted it to work, then, the will is a Medusa's head made of legal language. The collection itself suggests the analogy: the focal point of Fenway Court, the art object in the center of the center courtyard, is a Roman mosaic of the Medusa's head. In Greek mythology, the Medusa was one of the

8. Carter, op. cit., 188.

9. Ibid., 196–7.
10. Ibid., 175.

three Gorgons, but the only mortal among them. Her serpent hair and staring eyes literally petrified anyone who looked at them. Works of art usually depict her head alone, for Perseus managed to cut it off (cunningly looking at her in a mirror, not directly), thereafter using its powers for his own ends. He used the severed head to petrify Atlas, for example; later he gave the head to Athena as a gift, and she put it in the center of her shield. The Medusa's head, then, is the head of a dead woman, but death has not brought an end to her powers. At Fenway Court it sits as if on Athena's shield to remind trustees and visitors alike that Mrs. Gardner had a last will meant to last, a will to set her creation forever in stone.

Petrifaction or liquefaction: these are the options the will allows, and they bring us to one of that document's final details. Having said that if anyone tries to change the Museum it should be turned into money and the money given to Harvard, she adds in closing that in doing so, the art should be sold "in Paris, France." This is a nice touch, a last farewell to Puritan Boston, and another hint at how Mrs. Gardner imagined what she had created.

Like many of the rich museum builders of the late nineteenth and early twentieth centuries, Mrs. Gardner primarily assembled her creation from imported European art. In doing so, she was representative of American culture's broader post-Civil War shift away from republican simplicity and toward a New World version of aristocratic privilege. One might rightly say it was a shift toward class hierarchy, but those involved saw it differently. They saw it as opening America up to the kind of gentility, right behavior, and high art that republican government had trouble producing.

Nineteenth-century Americans traveling in Europe often came home convinced that a republican nation was incapable of producing magnificent art, magnificent buildings, or even well-behaved people. Here is George Hilliard, for example, writing in 1853, after a trip to Italy: "To bring a vast design to its ripe completion, requires perhaps the steady uniformity of monarchial institutions."[11] Or here an American doctor, Walter Channing, who spent a summer in Europe and then wrote a book to tell his countrymen how the common people of France, upon entering the Louvre, "put the shoes from off their feet, for they were on holy ground."[12] The French, Channing decided, knew how to behave because they had the Louvre; Americans had no Louvre and, thus, no manners.

In this way a talismanic civilizing influence was imputed to European art, and when that art was displayed in an American museum, "for the education and enjoyment of the public forever," it was with that influence in mind. William James, after attending the opening of the Museum, wrote Mrs. Gardner a thank-you note claiming that "the aesthetic perfection of all things . . . seemed to have a peculiar effect on the company, making them quiet and docile and self-forgetful and kind. . . . It was a very extra-ordinary and wonderful moral influence. . . . Quite in the line of a Gospel miracle!"[13] I actually don't know how much Mrs. Gardner herself saw the work that way. Maybe she used such rhetoric when it was useful to her and ignored it when it wasn't. Maybe William James was just being polite. Nonetheless, the will does seem to draw a line in the Atlantic and dare the trustees to cross it. If we take that seriously, then the collection can be imagined as a sort of "abduction of *Europa*" in the service of civilizing a new continent, and Mrs. Gardner's mention of Paris her way of saying that the talismans should be left in place to work their magic or else be carried back from whence they came and converted into coin. The trustees, of course, have chosen the former option. I imagine that at every meeting they cast their eyes upon the Medusa head so as to stiffen their resolve once more toward the task of keeping Mrs. Gardner's will in place.

In the summer of 1846, Henry Thoreau spent a night in jail for having refused to pay taxes he imagined going toward the support of slavery and a war with Mexico. "When I came out of prison," he later wrote, "I did not perceive that great changes had taken place on the common . . . ; and yet a change had to my eyes come over the scene."[14] In fantasy, at least, Thoreau stands on the common and sees both the state and his neighbors with new eyes. He sees that the people of the town "did not greatly propose to do right"; the state, he sees, "did not know its friends from its foes."[15]

Like the story out of Emerson with which I opened, Thoreau's "common moment" is not exactly democratic in its beginnings. Both

11. George Hilliard as quoted in Neil Harris, *The Artist in American Society* (New York: George Braziller, 1966), 158.
12. Walter Channing as quoted in ibid., 160.

13. William James as quoted in Carter, op. cit., 201.
14. Henry Thoreau, *Walden and Resistance to Civil Government*, second edition (New York: W. W. Norton, 1992), 240.
15. Ibid., 238.

moments might better be called autocratic, for each centers on a single man, a single self standing on the common and seeing the world freshly. The solitude of such epiphanies is only part of the story, however, for the fantasy of nineteenth-century social-spiritual life was that self-reliant individuals, given eyes to see, would see their way toward democracy. Thus did Walt Whitman believe, for example, that realized individuals would become democratic citizens, each of us being guided by a natural law of "adhesiveness or love, that fuses, ties and aggregates . . . , fraternizing all."[16]

These words come from "Democratic Vistas," an essay Whitman wrote after the Civil War because the vistas he imagined and hoped for were not the vistas he saw developing around him. After the Civil War, it became more and more apparent that no way existed to guarantee the fancied alchemy by which the common "I" is transmuted into the democratic or republican "we." It could as easily become a new version of the royal "we." Rich and poor may walk together on the commons in America, but if the point is that New World spaces are less rule-bound than their Old World antecedents, then ironically, the point is also that no single "vista" of America has privilege of place. Who is to say which is the real American way—a lavish display of entrepreneurial wealth or a Thoreauvian voluntary poverty? And who is to say whether contact with the divine should be mediated by the church, its traditions and its art, as Mrs. Gardner clearly preferred, or be face-to-face as Emerson hoped?

Mrs. Gardner had her own sense of how we are to see the true and the beautiful (not to mention the neighbors and the state), and in the land of free enterprise, the vista she offers is no less American than Whitman's or Emerson's. It even has its own version of adhesiveness, a New World version of community derived from precisely those traditions—"feudal and ecclesiastic"—that Whitman hoped we would abandon.[17] Fenway Court is a particularly American mix of entrepreneurial wealth and the spirit of the Stuart kings. It memorializes the sort of American individualism belonging to merchant princes and princesses, not to transcendentalist loners. It is animated not so much by the spirit of New England's "bare common[s]" as by the ghost of a commons older and more feudal. I say "ghost" because that commons can never return in fact, the merchant princes having had to kill it before they themselves could come to power (true aristocrats never having stooped to trade). Our hostess at the Gardner Museum may have carried a torch for Charles I, and dressed her work in Mary Stuart's silks, but the power that made that dressing up possible did not come down from King Fergus I, it came from New World railroads, imported linen, and an iron mine outside Uniontown, Pennsylvania.

This is not to say we have come to the end of the story. Luckily, we never shall. The double meaning of Mrs. Gardner's *plaisir* means that visitors will always enter who find pleasures and learning not stinted by the Order of the White Rose. The lady had good lawyers, but it is very hard to command the future after death, even should they let you write your will in stone. When Perseus came to the Medusa's home in the Land of the Hyperboreans, he found her among the rain-worn shapes of the men and wild beasts she had petrified.[18] Mark that "rain-worn": stone itself weathers away over time. The will may well control future trustees, but it cannot really control the space. Fenway Court was built on the Fenway in Boston, and the Fenway was created from a fen, a bog, a swamp, which is why the mosaic of the Medusa's head, originally installed level with the surrounding courtyard, has sunk four and a half feet. Thieves, too, have broken in and removed paintings without waking those Harvard lawyers. Moreover, Mrs. Gardner's will omitted a few parts of the building, including the rooms at the back, where Lee Mingwei has organized a project that may prompt us toward new, twenty-first-century answers to the questions I posed at the outset. What does it mean to invite someone into your home to see your art? What sort of space is created when you quit that home and leave it to the public?

Lewis Hyde

16. Walt Whitman, "Democratic Vistas," in *Prose Works 1892*, Floyd Stovall, ed. (New York: New York University Press, 1963–64), 381.
17. Ibid., 364.
18. See Robert Graves, *The Greek Myths*, vol. 1 (New York: George Braziller, 1957), 239.

LEE MINGWEI

Day 28 13:21 Eating with Lily

Day 29 09:40 Meditating with Lily

Day 30 14:48 Crying with Lily

Day 31 21:56 Writing with Lily

Day 32 19:43 Shopping with Lily

Day 33 09:23 Eating with Lily

Day 34 17:26 Cooking with Lily

Day 35 19:39 Masturbating with Lily

Day 36 12:34 Eating with Lily

Day 37 09:19 Riding with Lily

Day 38 10:20 Talking with Lily

Day 39 12:43 Cooking with Lily

Day 40 13:41 Eating with Lily

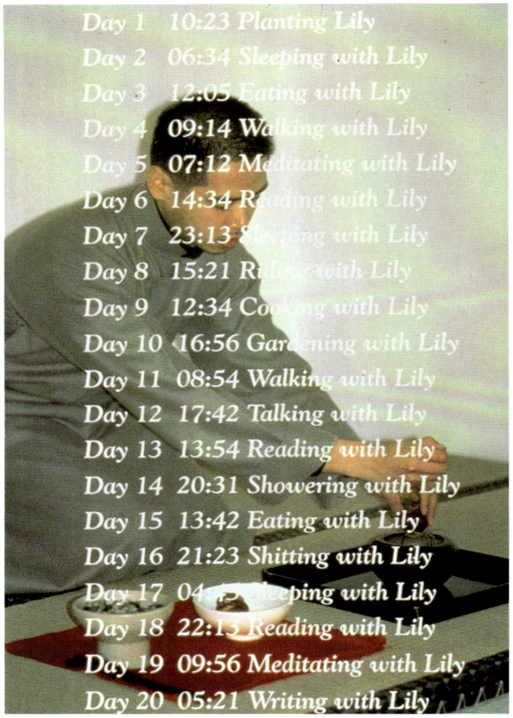

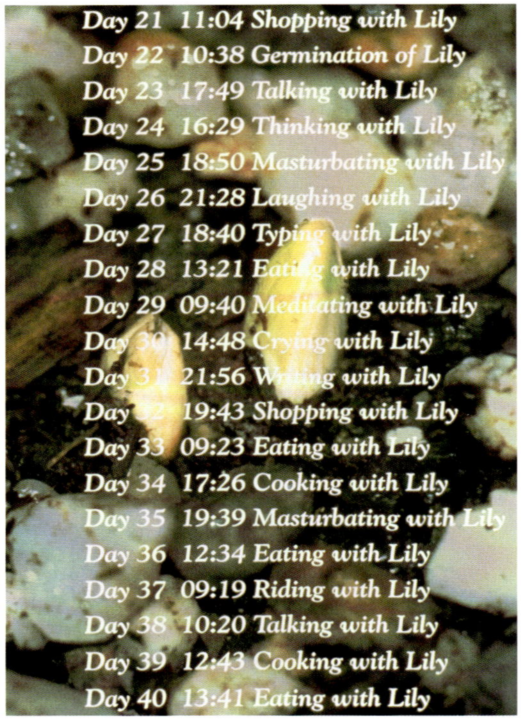

100 Days with Lily #1–#5 1995 silver dye bleach prints (Ilfochrome) 20 x 16 inches each Courtesy of Lombard/Freid Fine Art, New York, New York
Previous page: Detail, image # 2.

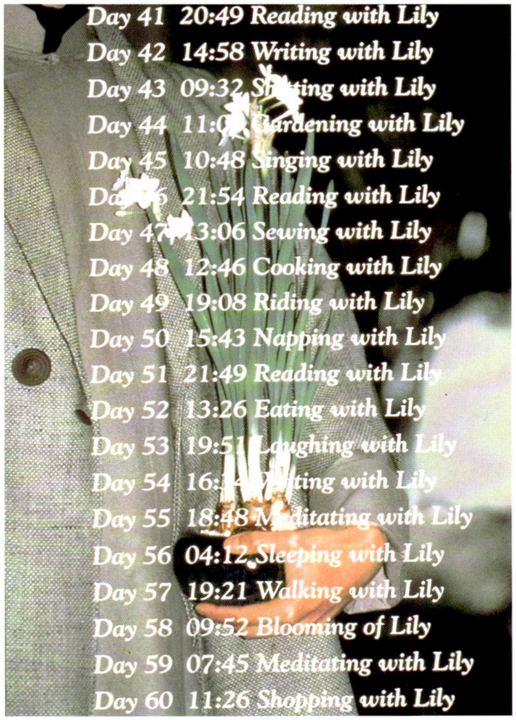
Day 41 20:49 Reading with Lily
Day 42 14:58 Writing with Lily
Day 43 09:32 with Lily
Day 44 with Lily
Day 45 10:48 with Lily
Day 21:54 Reading with Lily
Day 47 3:06 Sewing with Lily
Day 48 12:46 Cooking with Lily
Day 49 19:08 Riding with Lily
Day 50 15:43 Napping with Lily
Day 51 21:49 Reading with Lily
Day 52 13:26 Eating with Lily
Day 53 19:51 with Lily
Day 54 with Lily
Day 55 18:48 with Lily
Day 56 04:12 Sleeping with Lily
Day 57 19:21 Walking with Lily
Day 58 09:52 Blooming of Lily
Day 59 07:45 Meditating with Lily
Day 60 11:26 Shopping with Lily

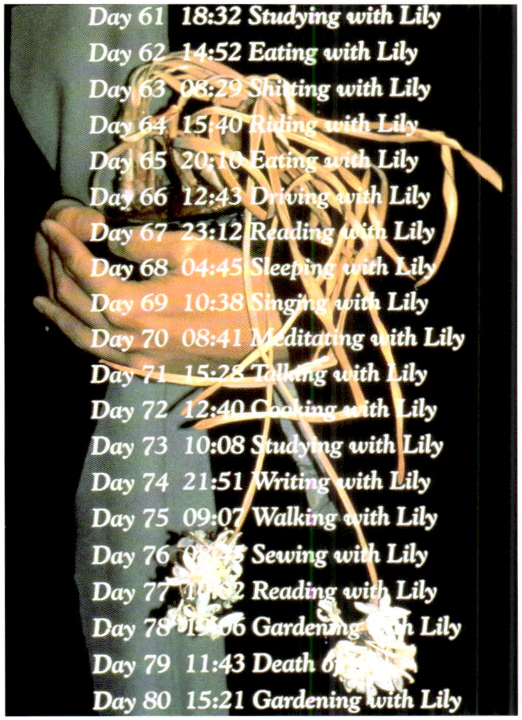
Day 61 18:32 Studying with Lily
Day 62 14:52 Eating with Lily
Day 63 08:29 with Lily
Day 64 15:40 Riding with Lily
Day 65 with Lily
Day 66 12:43 with Lily
Day 67 23:12 Reading with Lily
Day 68 04:45 Sleeping with Lily
Day 69 10:38 Singing with Lily
Day 70 08:41 with Lily
Day 71 with Lily
Day 72 12:40 with Lily
Day 73 10:08 with Lily
Day 74 21:51 Writing with Lily
Day 75 Walking with Lily
Day 76 Sewing with Lily
Day 77 Reading with Lily
Day 78 Lily
Day 79 11:43 Death
Day 80 15:21 Gardening with Lily

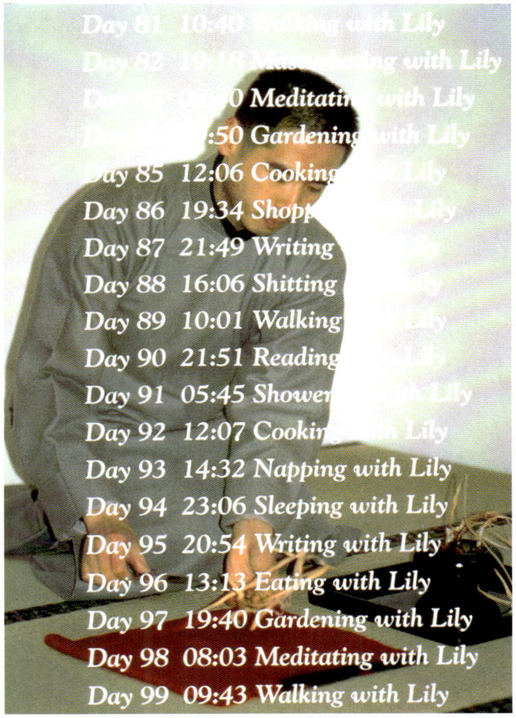
Day 81 10:40 with Lily
Day 82 with Lily
Meditati with Lily
:50 Gardening with Lily
Day 85 12:06 Cooking
Day 86 19:34
Day 87 21:49 Writing
Day 88 16:06 Shitting
Day 89 10:01 Walking
Day 90 21:51 Reading
Day 91 05:45
Day 92 12:07
Day 93 14:32 Napping with Lily
Day 94 23:06 Sleeping with Lily
Day 95 20:54 Writing with Lily
Day 96 13:13 Eating with Lily
Day 97 19:40 Gardening with Lily
Day 98 08:03 Meditating with Lily
Day 99 09:43 Walking with Lily

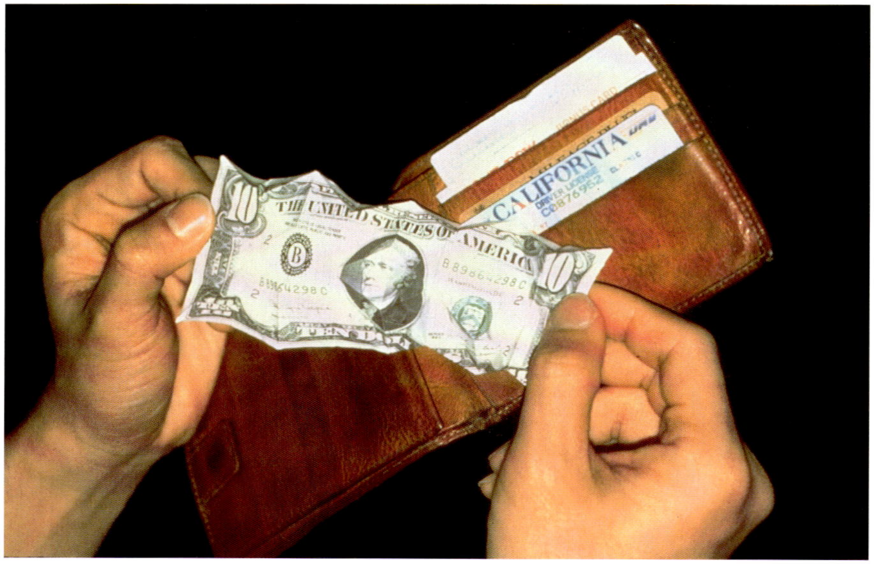

Money for Art #1–#5 1994 silver dye bleach prints (Ilfochrome) 11 x 14 inches each Courtesy of Lombard/Freid Fine Art, New York, New York

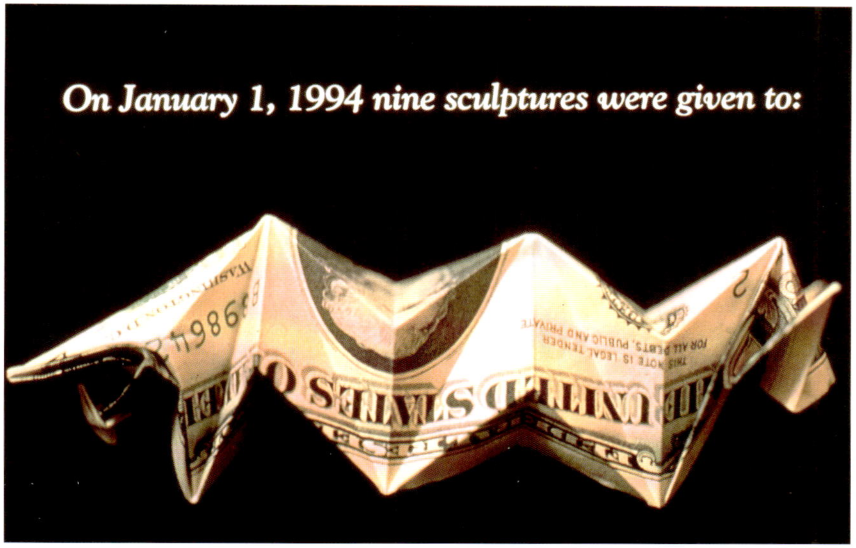
On January 1, 1994 nine sculptures were given to:

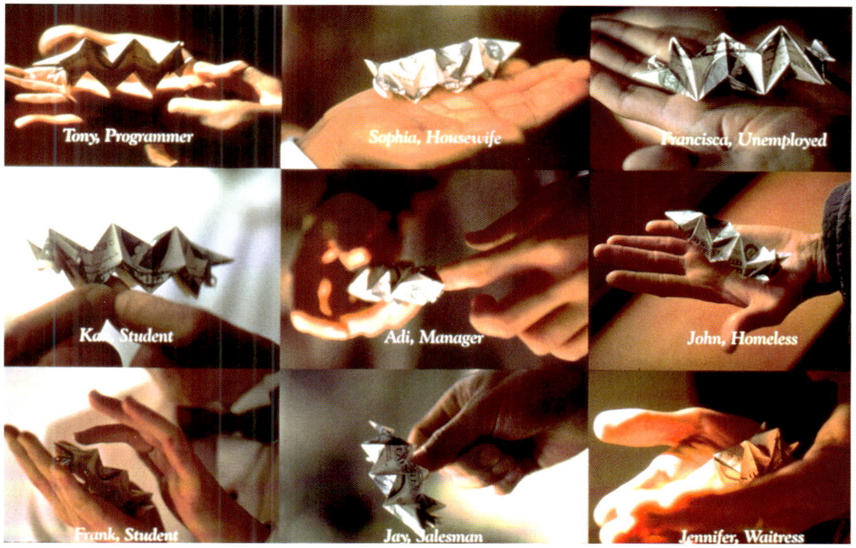
Tony, Programmer
Sophia, Housewife
Francisca, Unemployed
Student
Adi, Manager
John, Homeless
Frank, Student
Jay, Salesman
Jennifer, Waitress

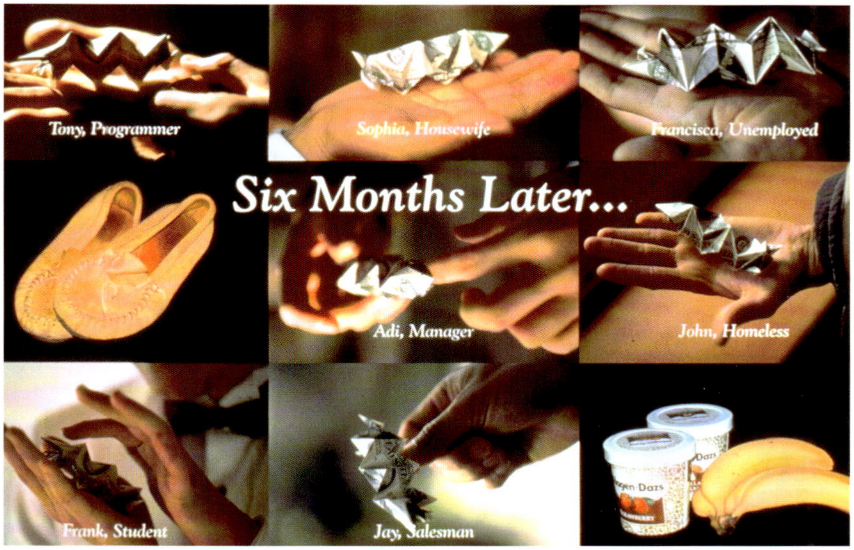
Tony, Programmer
Sophia, Housewife
Francisca, Unemployed
Six Months Later...
Adi, Manager
John, Homeless
Frank, Student
Jay, Salesman

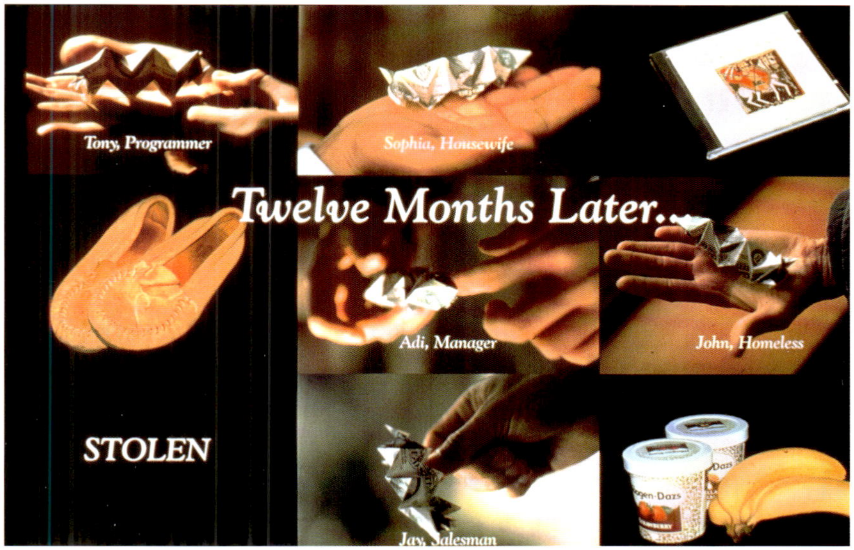
Tony, Programmer
Sophia, Housewife
Twelve Months Later...
Adi, Manager
John, Homeless
STOLEN
Jay, Salesman

30 *Money for Art* 1997 wood, shelving, origami sculpture from U.S. currency, traded objects 59 x 58 x 5 inches (each shelving unit)
Courtesy of Lombard/Freid Fine Art, New York, New York

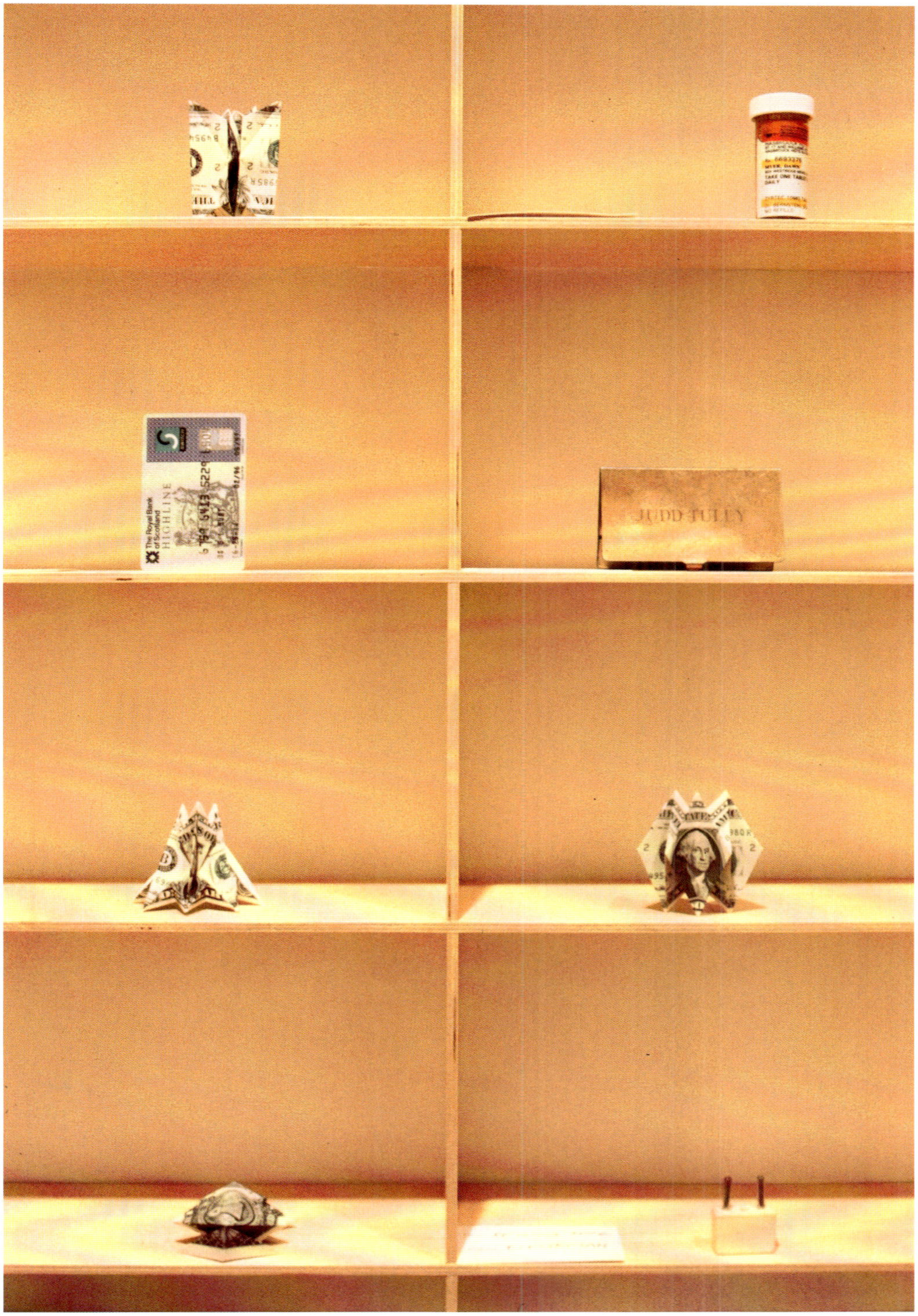
JUDD TULLY

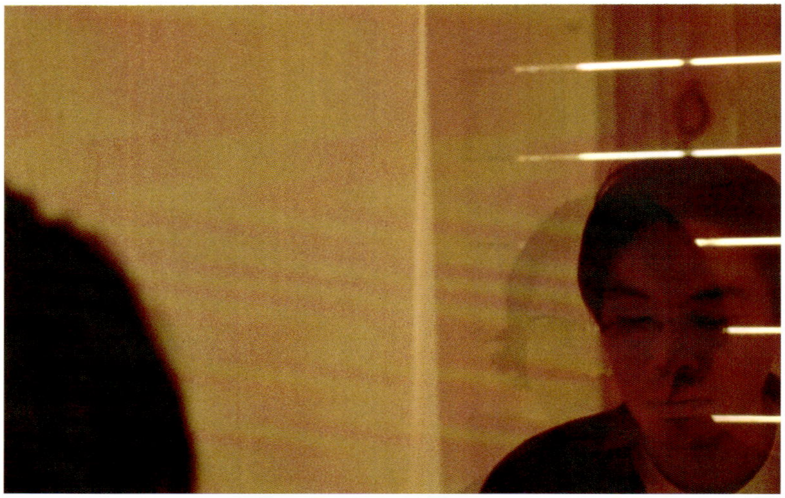

Reflection 1997 wood, muslin, two-way mirror 108 x 144 x 36 inches Courtesy of Mr. Glory Yeh

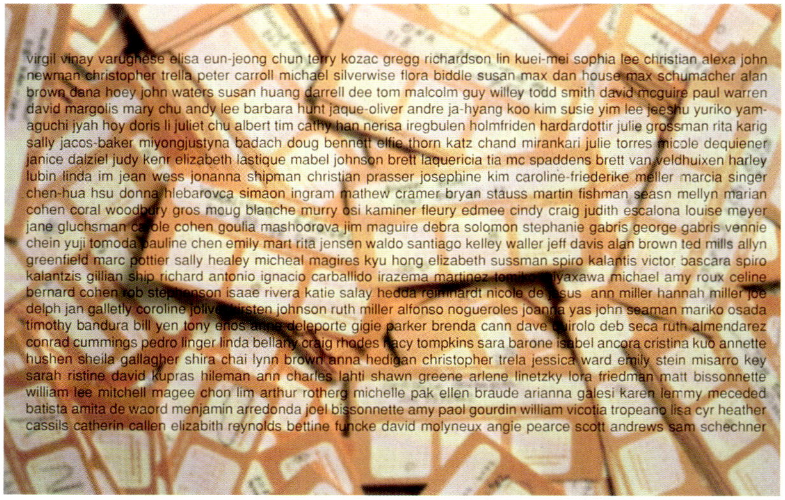

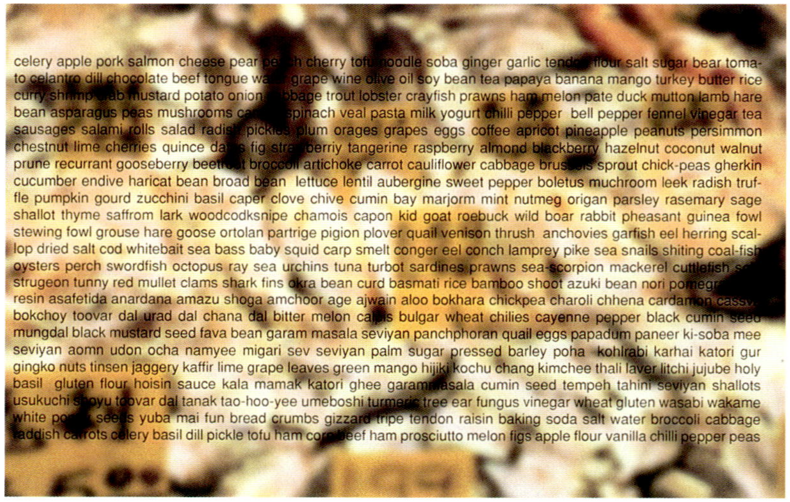

The Dining Project 1997 wood, audiotape players, beans, rice, tatami mats 132 x 132 x 24 inches
Courtesy of The Whitney Museum of American Art, New York, New York

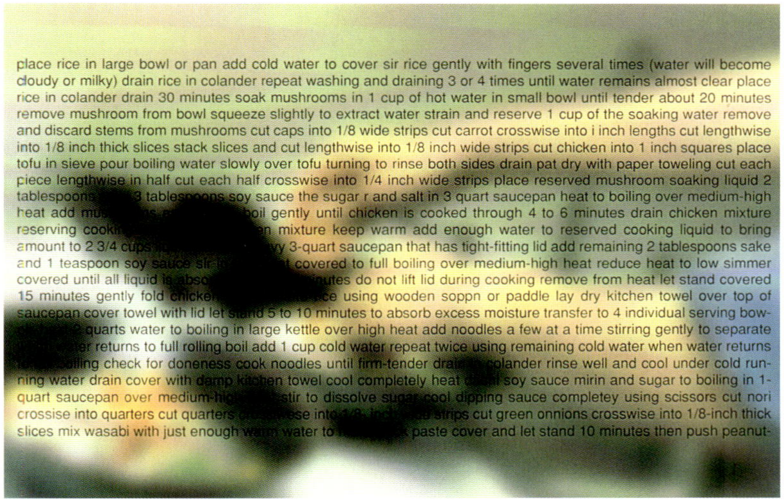
place rice in large bowl or pan add cold water to cover sir rice gently with fingers several times (water will become
cloudy or milky) drain rice in colander repeat washing and draining 3 or 4 times until water remains almost clear place
rice in colander drain 30 minutes soak mushrooms in 1 cup of hot water in small bowl until tender about 20 minutes
remove mushroom from bowl squeeze slightly to extract water strain and reserve 1 cup of the soaking water remove
and discard stems from mushrooms cut caps into 1/8 wide strips cut carrot crosswise into i inch lengths cut lengthwise
into 1/8 inch thick slices stack slices and cut lengthwise into 1/8 inch wide strips cut chicken into 1 inch squares place
tofu in sieve pour boiling water slowly over tofu turning to rinse both sides drain pat dry with paper toweling cut each
piece lengthwise in half cut each half crosswise into 1/4 inch wide strips place reserved mushroom soaking liquid 2
tablespoons 3 tablespoons soy sauce the sugar r and salt in 3 quart saucepan heat to boiling over medium-high
heat add boil gently until chicken is cooked through 4 to 6 minutes drain chicken mixture
reserving mixture keep warm add enough water to reserved cooking liquid to bring
amount to 2 3/4 cups 3-quart saucepan that has tight-fitting lid add remaining 2 tablespoons sake
and 1 teaspoon soy covered to full boiling over medium-high heat reduce heat to low simmer
covered until all liquid do not lift lid during cooking remove from heat let stand covered
15 minutes gently fold using wooden soppn or paddle lay dry kitchen towel over top of
saucepan cover towel with lid let 5 to 10 minutes to absorb excess moisture transfer to 4 individual serving bow-
quarts water to boiling in large kettle over high heat add noodles a few at a time stirring gently to separate
returns to full rolling boil add 1 cup cold water repeat twice using remaining cold water when water returns
check for doneness cook noodles until firm-tender colander rinse well and cool under cold run-
ning water drain cover with damp kitchen towel cool completely heat soy sauce mirin and sugar to boiling in 1-
quart saucepan over medium- stir to dissolve cool dipping sauce completey using scissors cut nori
crossise into quarters cut quarters strips cut green onnions crosswise into 1/8-inch thick
slices mix wasabi with just enough water to paste cover and let stand 10 minutes then push peanut-

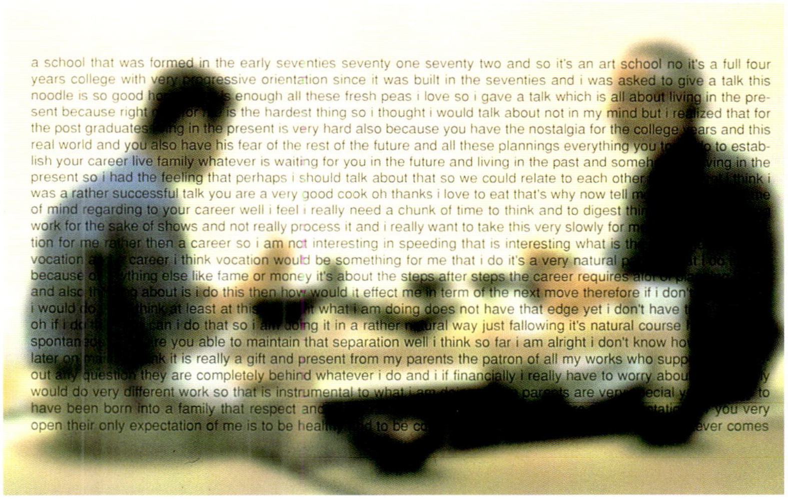
a school that was formed in the early seventies seventy one seventy two and so it's an art school no it's a full four
years college with progressive orientation since it was built in the seventies and i was asked to give a talk this
noodle is so good enough all these fresh peas i love so i gave a talk which is all about living in the pre-
sent because right is the hardest thing so i thought i would talk about not in my mind but i realized that for
the post graduates in the present is very hard also because you have the nostalgia for the college ears and this
real world and you also have his fear of the rest of the future and all these plannings everything you to estab-
lish your career live family whatever is waiting for you in the future and living in the past and some ving in the
present so i had the feeling that perhaps i should talk about that so we could relate to each other think i
was a rather successful talk you are a very good cook oh thanks i love to eat that's why now tell
of mind regarding to your career well i feel i really need a chunk of time to think and to digest
work for the sake of shows and not really process it and i really want to take this very slowly for
tion for me rather then a career so i am not interesting in speeding that is interesting what is
vocation career i think vocation would be something for me that i do it's a very natural
because thing else like fame or money it's about the steps after steps the career requires
and also about is i do this then how would it effect me in term of the next move therefore if i don
i would think at least at this what i am doing does not have that edge yet i don't have
oh if i can i do that so i doing it in a rather way just fallowing it's natural course
spontan you able to maintain that separation well i think so far i am alright i don't know ho
later on it is really a gift and present from my parents the patron of all my works who supp
out they are completely behind whatever i do and i if financially i really have to worry abou
would do very different work so that is instrumental to parents are very ecial to
have been born into a family that respect and you very
open their only expectation of me is to be heal to be ever comes

The Dining Project 1997 wood, audiotape players, beans, rice, tatami mats 132 x 132 x 24 inches
Courtesy of The Whitney Museum of American Art, New York, New York

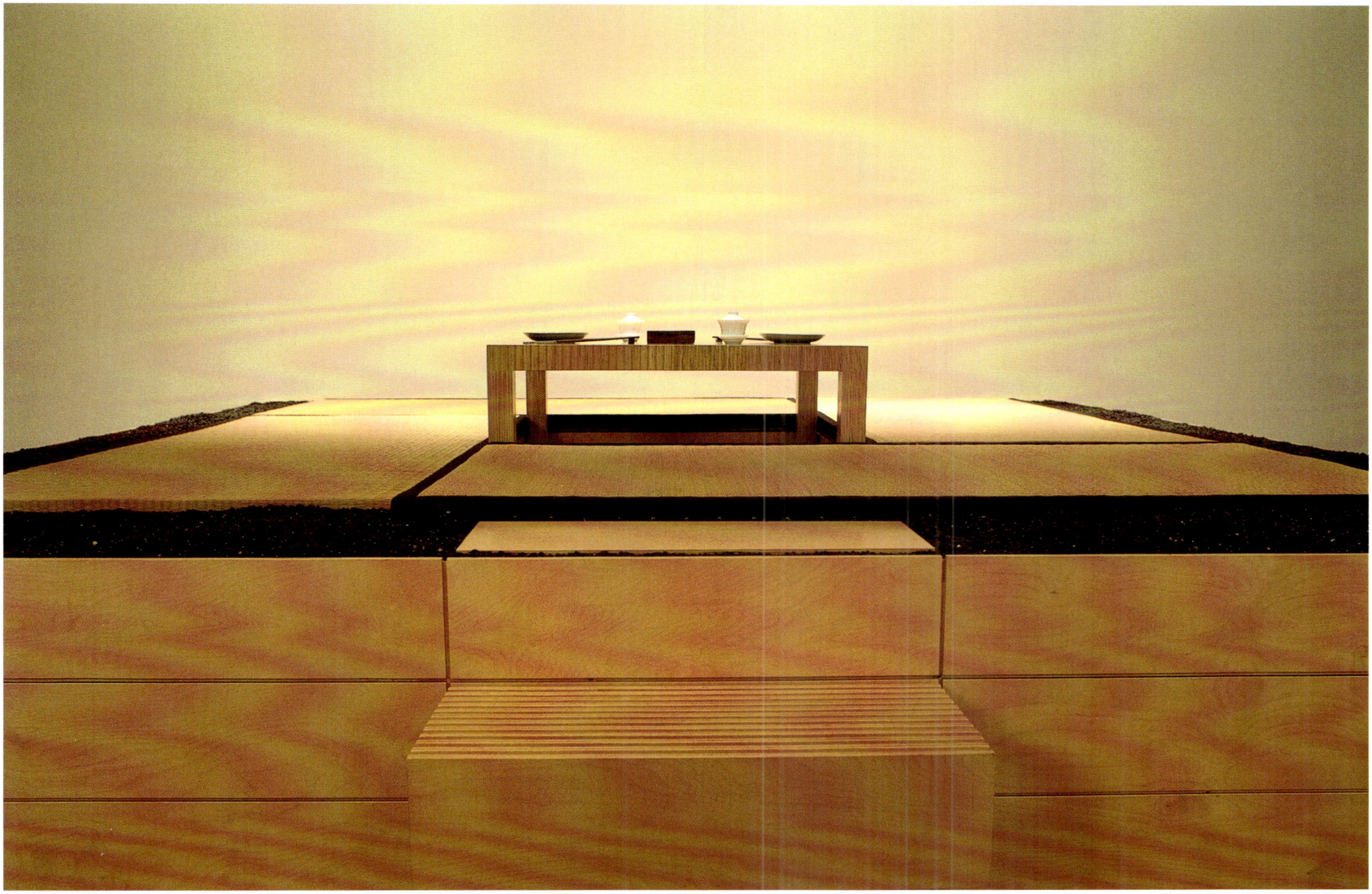

The Letter Writing Project (detail) 1998 wood, glass, paper 114 x 67 x 91 inches
Courtesy of The Whitney Museum of American Art, New York, New York; and the The Fabric Workshop and Museum, Philadelphia, Pennsylvania

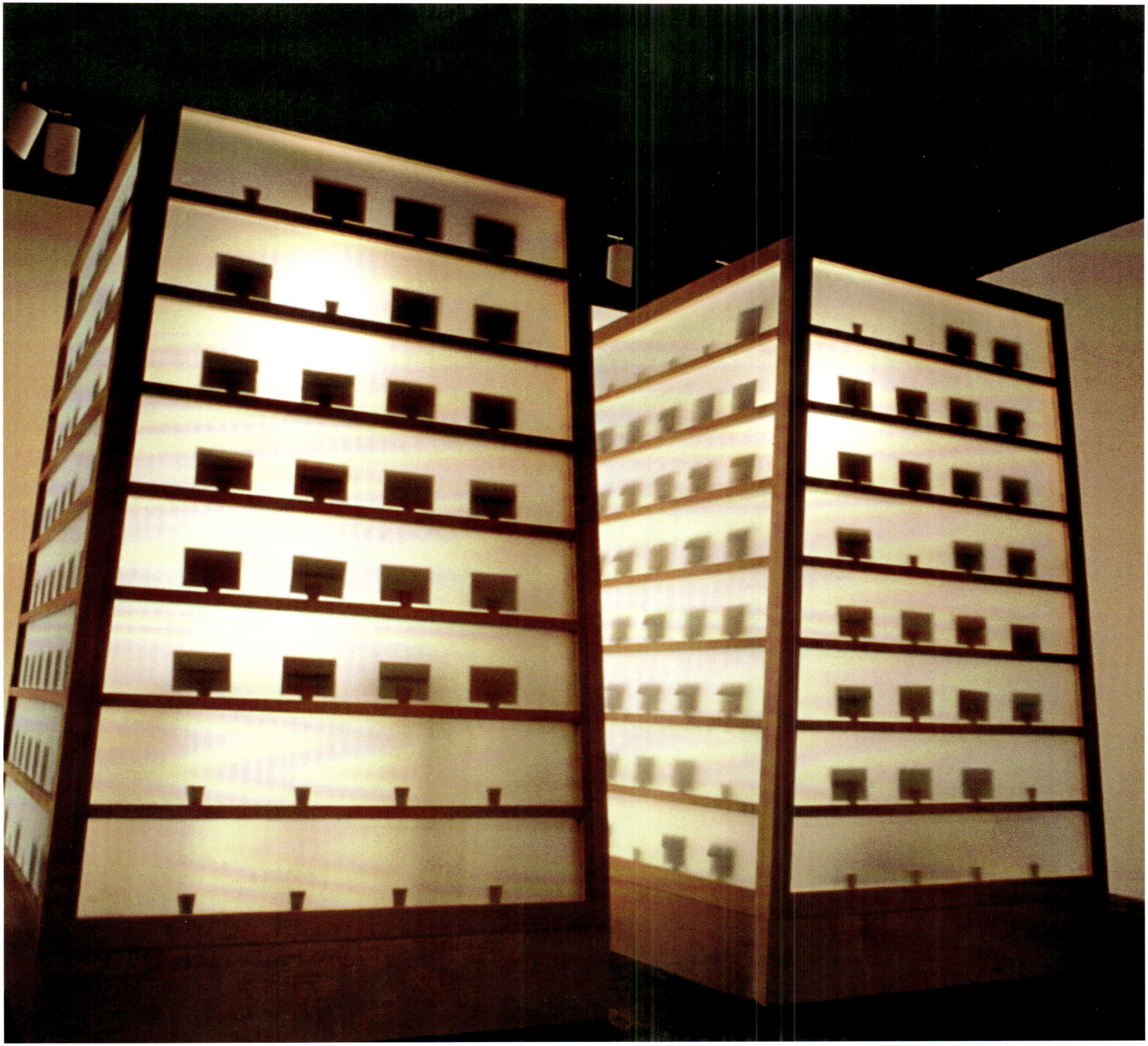

40 *The Letter Writing Project* 1998 wood, glass, paper 114 x 67 x 91 inches
Courtesy of The Whitney Museum of American Art, New York, New York; and the The Fabric Workshop and Museum, Philadelphia, Pennsylvania

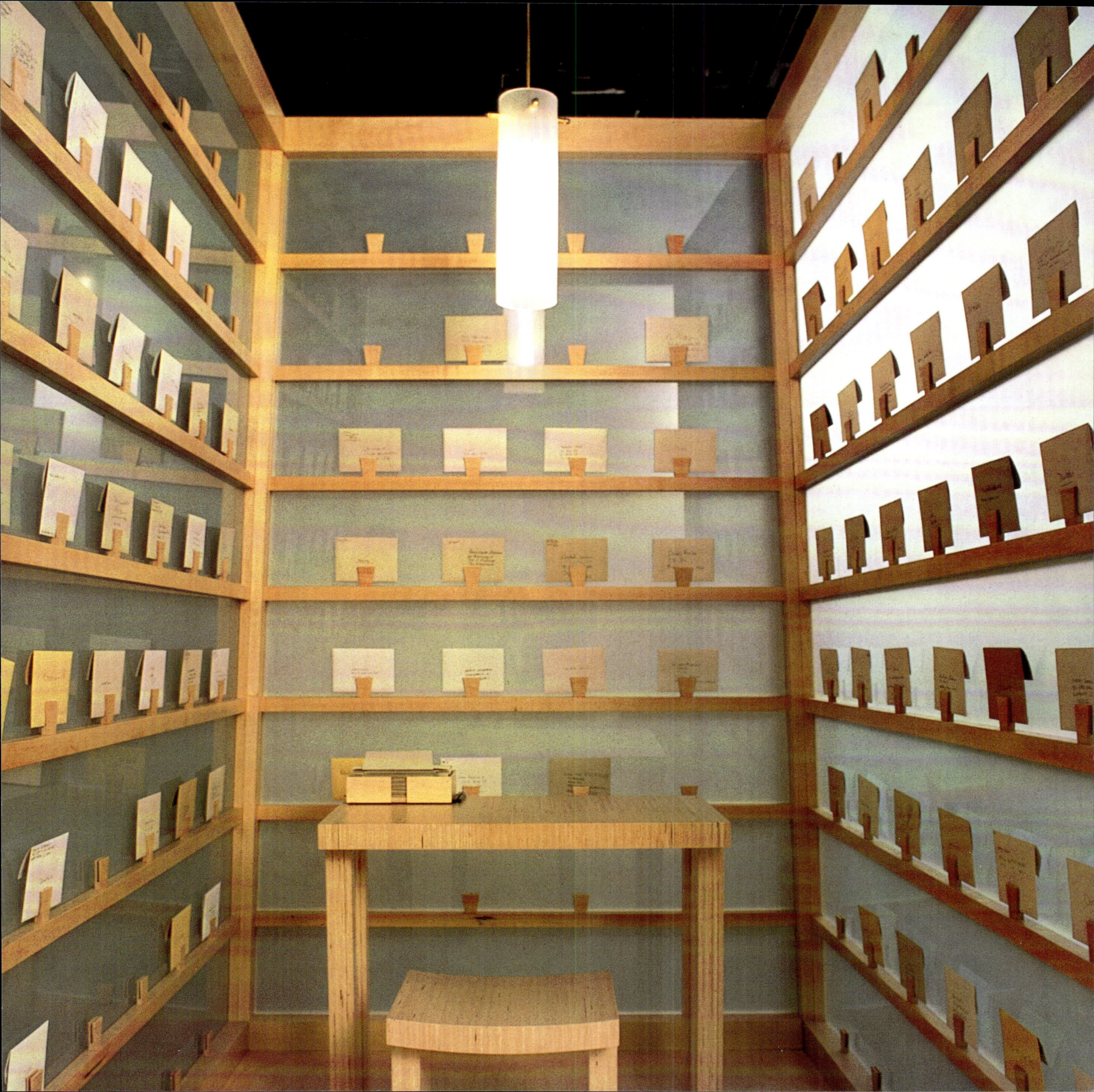

42 *The Living Room* Project (installation view) 2000 mixed media dimensions variable
Isabella Stewart Gardner Museum

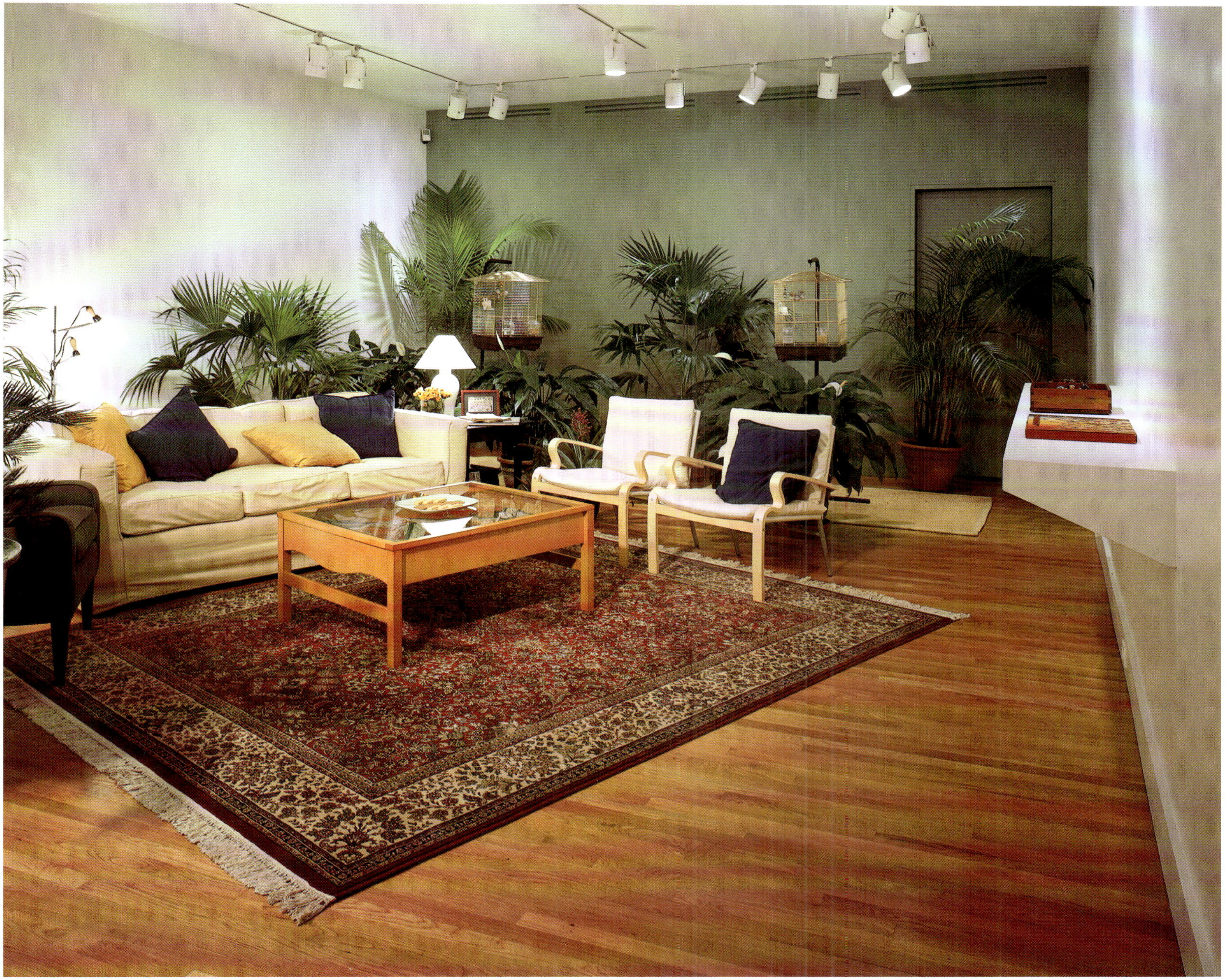

44 *The Living Room* (detail) 2000 mixed media dimensions variable
Isabella Stewart Gardner Museum

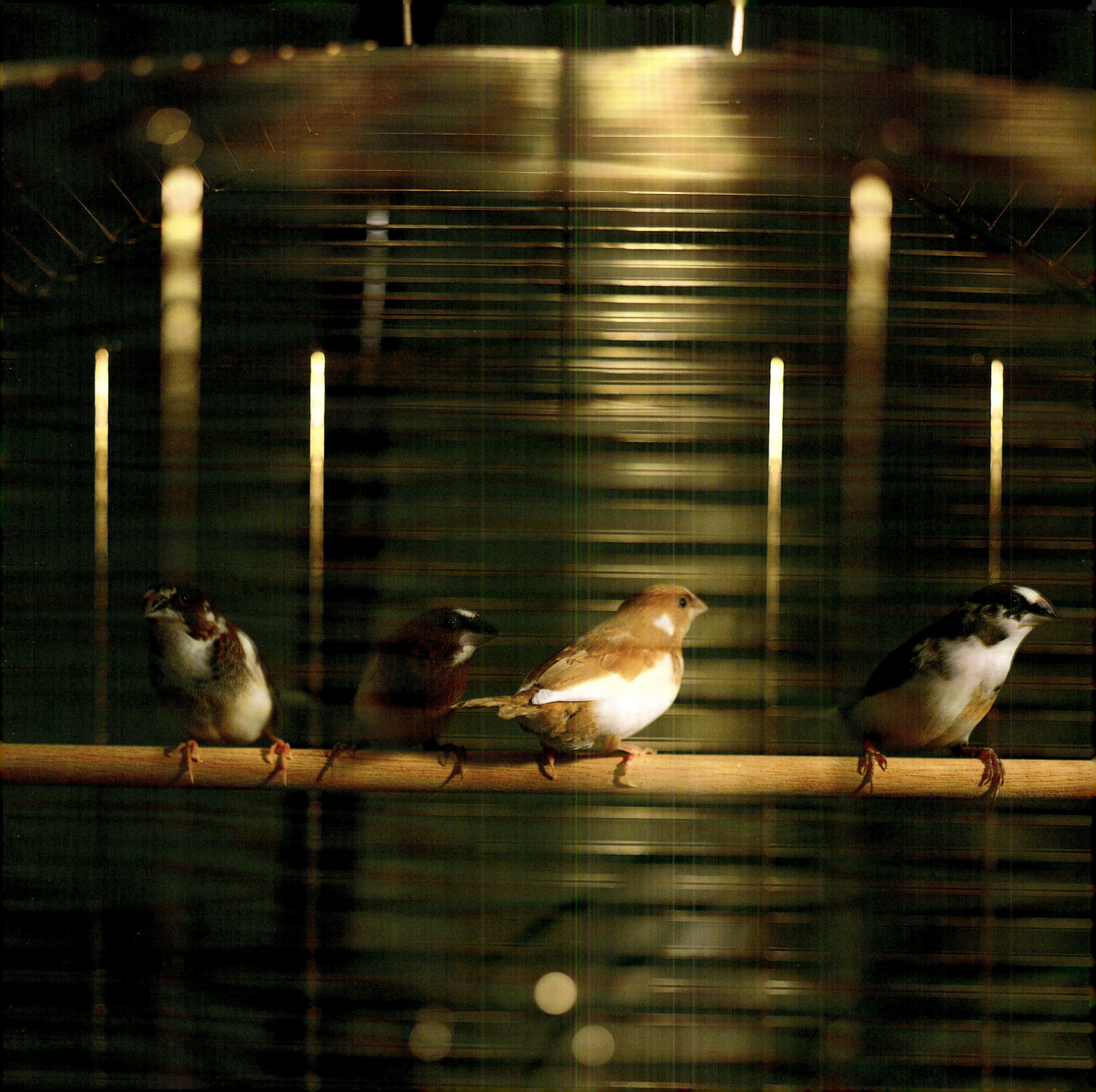

LEE MINGWEI: BIOGRAPHICAL INFORMATION

1964 Born in Taiwan

EDUCATION

1995–97 Yale University, New Haven, Connecticut. Graduate School of Fine Arts. M.F.A. in sculpture, concentrating in new genre public art

1989–93 California College of Arts and Crafts, Oakland, California. B.F.A. with honors, textile arts

1991 Haystack Mountain School of Craft, Deer Isle, Maine. Weaving with Lia Cook

1987–88 University of Hawaii at Manoa. Studies in architecture

ARTIST IN RESIDENCE

2000 Headlands Center for Contemporary Art, Sausalito, California

1999 Acadia Summer Arts Program, Mount Desert Isle, Maine
Isabella Stewart Gardner Museum, Boston, Massachusetts

SOLO EXHIBITIONS

2000 *The Living Room,* Isabella Stewart Gardner Museum, Boston, Massachusetts

Empathic Economies, Davis Museum, Wellesley College, Wellesley, Massachusetts; Fort Lauderdale Museum for Contemporary Art, Fort Lauderdale, Florida

1999 *Lee Mingwei*: *1994–1999*, Cleveland Center for Contemporary Art, Cleveland, Ohio

1998 *The Letter Writing Project,* Fabric Workshop and Museum, Philadelphia, Pennsylvania

Way Stations (Contemporary Art Series), Whitney Museum of American Art, New York, New York

1997 *InteractExchange*, Lombard/Freid Fine Arts, New York, New York

GROUP EXHIBITIONS

1999 *Meaning to Write* (special version of *The Letter Writing Project*), Third Asia Pacific Triennial of Contemporary Art, Queensland Art Gallery, Brisbane, Australia

1998 *Plural Speech*, White Box, New York, New York

100 Days with Lily, Weatherspoon Art Gallery, Greensboro, North Carolina

1997 *Money for Art*, Refusalon, San Francisco, California

The World View, Deutsche Bank, New York, New York

Reflections (graduate thesis project), Graduate Art & Architecture Gallery, Yale University, New Haven, Connecticut

1993 *Lee Mingwei*, Oliver Art Gallery, California College of Arts and Crafts, Oakland, California

PRESS

1999 "My Dinner with Mingwei," *Northern Ohio Live*. Rice Hershey

"The Buddhist Way," by Frank Green, *Cleveland Free Times*, review of *Lee Mingwei: 1994–1999*, Cleveland Center for Contemporary Art, Cleveland, Ohio

"Artist Extends an Invitation to Look Inside," by Steven Litt, *Cleveland Plain Dealer*, review of *Lee Mingwei: 1994–1999*, Cleveland Center for Contemporary Art, Cleveland, Ohio

Interview with Dee Perry on "Around Noon," WCPN, Cleveland, Ohio

"Dining Gallery: At Museums across the Country, Lee Mingwei Merges Food and Art," by Alan Brown, *Food & Wine*

1998 "Between Heaven and Hell," by Robin Rice, *Philadelphia City Paper*, review of Fabric Workshop exhibition

"Transforming Death's Wound: A Healing Art," by Kay Larson, *New York Times*

"Letter Writing as Art and a Devotional," by Edward J. Sozanski, *Philadelphia Enquirer*

"Four Projects, Four Experiences," by Yeh I-Lan, *Vogue* (Chinese edition)

Ninety: Art des Années 90/Art in the 90's 29, issue devoted to Gerhard Richter and Lee Mingwei. Charenton Cedex, France

"My Dinner with Ming-Wei," by Carol Kino, *Time Out New York* 145

"The Zen of Listening," by Mei Chen, *A. Magazine: Inside Asian America*

"Subject X—Notes on Performative Art: Part I," by Barry Schwabsky, *Art+Text* 60

1997 "Ming-Wei Lee," by Eileen Myles, *Art in America*

"Performance Art," by Chen Chin-Chin, *United Daily*, TAIWAN, ROC

"Money for Art," by Lucas Lin, *World Journal* (international Chinese-language daily)

"Surprises," by Elayne Lebre, *Elle* (French edition)

"Money for Art," by Hsieh Hui-Ching, *Ming Pao Daily News*

"The Dining Project," interview with Carol Zimmer, NBC Radio, New York, New York

"The Dining Project," interview with Tessa Sprawl, CBC Radio, Canada

"Museum Preserves Dinner Dialogue," by Beth Gardiner, Associated Press news release

Interview with Laura Sydell on "Morning Edition," WNYC, New York, New York

"The Dining Project," Stefan Jones, SJS Radio, USA

"Ming-Wei Lee, 'InteractExchange,'" by Anne Doran, *Time Out New York* 93, review of Lombard/Freid exhibition

"Voice Choices, Galleries, Especially Recommended," by Kim Levin, *Village Voice*, review of Lombard/Freid exhibition

"The Success of the Dining Project," by Vivian Wu, *World Journal* (international Chinese–language daily)

Chin Wu-Tsieh, *Ming Pao Daily News*, review of InteractExchange exhibition at Lombard/Freid Gallery, New York, New York

"Artist of the Everyday," by Catherine Gysin Lamont, *Utne Reader*

1996

"The Dining Project: The Art of Nurturing," by Lee Mingwei, *Tricycle: The Buddhist Review*

NOTE: Numerous reviews and articles have also run in Chinese newspapers, periodicals, and art journals, especially in Taiwan.

HONORS

1999 Second-place award for Web site *malepregnancy.com*, collaborative project with Virgil Wong, New York, New York, *New Media* magazine

Recent Graduate of Distinction Award, California College of Arts and Crafts, Oakland, California

1997 Joan Mitchell Foundation Grant

PUBLIC COLLECTIONS

Deutsche Bank, New York, New York

Weatherspoon Art Gallery, Greensboro, North Carolina

Whitney Museum of American Art, New York, New York,

Yageo Art Foundation, Taipei, Taiwan

ABOUT THE AUTHORS

Jennifer R. Gross is curator of contemporary art and public programs at the Gardner Museum. Previously she was director of the Institute of Contemporary Art at the Maine College of Art in Portland, Maine. Gross obtained a Ph.D. in nineteenth- and twentieth-century European and American painting and sculpture from the City University of New York, Graduate Center, in 1999. The American artist Richard Tuttle was the subject of her dissertation.

Lewis Hyde is the author of two books on creativity, *The Gift* (1983) and *Trickster Makes This World* (1998). A MacArthur Fellow, he teaches at Kenyon College, in Ohio, where he is the Luce Professor of Art and Politics.

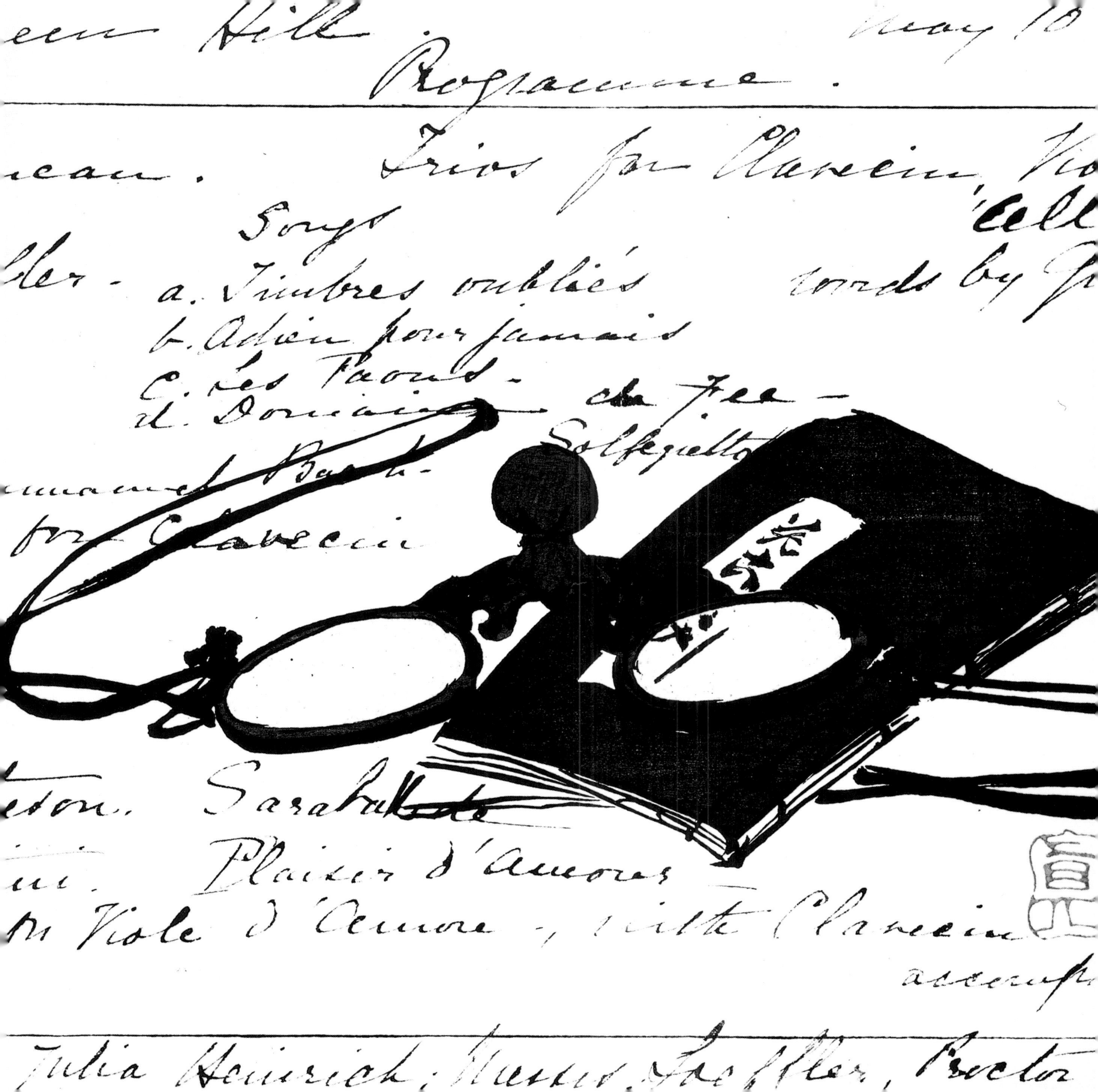

Programme.
Trios for Clavecin,
'Cell
Songs
a. Timbres oubliés
b. Adieu pour jamais
c. Les Paons
words by
Solfegietto
Bach
for Clavecin
Sarabande
Plaisir d'Amour
Viole d'Amour, with Clavecin
accomp
Julia Heinrich, Proctor

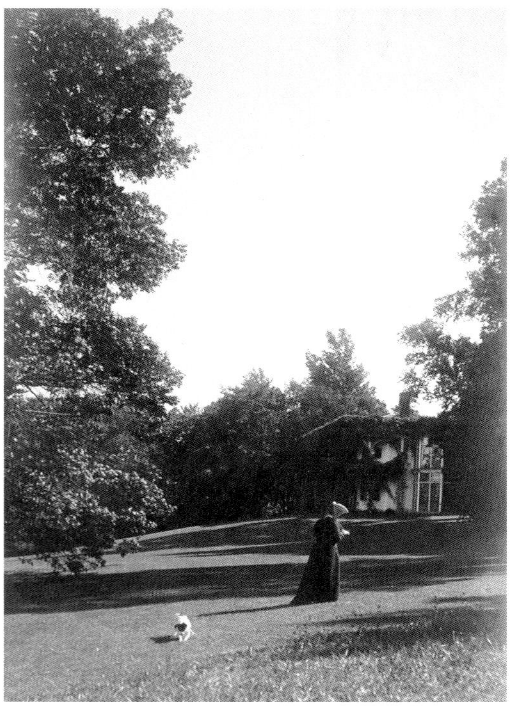